INTERNATIONAL FOOTBA

No. 31

'STROLLER' GRAHAM was his nickname in his
playing days. Now he's 'Smiler' Graham—and Arsenal
manager has plenty to smile about as he clutches the
League Championship trophies, back at Highbury
after far too long.

INTERNATIONAL FOOTBALL BOOK No. 31

Edited by
Hallam Gordon

SOUVENIR PRESS LTD · LONDON

ISBN 0 258 62958 1

COVER PICTURES

PRIDE of place to Peter Shilton, in all his goalkeeper's finery, on becoming the most-capped Englishman. Cover recognition also for David O'Leary, long-serving member of the Arsenal title-winning team.

Filmset and printed in England
by BAS Printers Limited, Over Wallop, Hampshire

FINAL GLORY

THEY'RE falling about laughing— and for good reason. Jubilant Celtic get together with the Scottish Cup after beating the old enemy Rangers in the 1989 Final.

PROUD moment for Ronnie Whelan, the Liverpool captain, as he lifts the FA Cup after his side had beaten their old enemy Everton 3–2 after extra time.

CAPITAL CITY

Contents

	Page
Capital City of Soccer, by Mick Demuth	6
Beware of the Bull! by Brendan Gallagher	13
Big Jack and his Jolly Green Giants, by Des Kelly	16
Wilkins is pick of the Scots	23
Two 'firsts' for Brazilian aces, by John Price	27
World Cup 1990 . . . Italy beckons, by Keir Radnedge	30
Peter Shilton . . . business as usual, by Alastair Yeomans	38
Glenn Hysen, Liverpool and Sweden, by Ian Cruise	43
Scapegoat Mark Huges is back on top, by Des Kelly	45
A new rival for Real	49
Gunners at the double! by Mark Demuth	52
Football history for Pizanti and Israel, by Peter Drury	59
Dean of Derby is up with the stars	61
Michel magic, by John Price	64
Mechelen riding high again	68
Bobby is back where he belongs, by Dennis Signy OBE	71
Blue is the colour, by Bryon Butler	76
This is your life, John Toshack! by Alex Spink	78
Jim Leighton under the microscope, by Jason Tomas	83
Home-bread skills of Jurgen Klinsmann, by Mark Demuth	86
Paul Gascoigne . . . genius or joker? by Alastair Yeomans	90
IFB salutes Steve Nicol	95
The horror of Hillsborough	98
Argentina in hat-trick bid, by Keir Radnedge	101
Fergie's Fledglings, by Des Kelly	104
The man who made United great, by Donald Saunders	109
Lawyer Gudni's trial is over, by Peter Drury	113
Russians look ahead	118
Nat's fifty years of devotion, by Mike Nally	119
The day Morty got it wrong, by William Johnson	120
The star who divided a city, by Jason Tomas	123
Women's football is alive and well, by Brendan Gallagher	127

OF SOCCER

The twin giants of San Siro stadium have shaken off the shackles says MARK DEMUTH (Sunday Express)

FIFA's decision to open the 1990 World Cup Finals in the magnificent San Siro stadium, Milan, on June 8 has proved an inspired choice. It would be difficult to imagine a more appropriate or more intoxicating venue for Argentina's first defence of the trophy they won in Mexico City.

Quite simply, Milan has emerged as the soccer capital of the world. At the start of season 1989–90, the Italian city contemplated occupying centre stage for the twelve months ahead.

In less than two seasons, the two clubs that share San Siro's splendid facili-

OPPOSITE Lothar Matthaus of West Germany, inspiration of Inter Milan in their 1989 Italian League championship triumph.

BELOW The imposing San Siro stadium which houses AC Milan and Internazionale and the first venue in the 1990 World Cup Finals.

ties, Internazionale and Milan, have shaken off shackles and pressures imposed by former glories to re-establish themselves as the leading protagonists of Italian football, with European domination beckoning.

Milan instigated the city's resurgence with an astonishing £8 million outlay on Dutch stars Ruud Gullit and Marco Van Basten in 1987. The boldness of the club's president, Silvio Berlusconi, and coach Arrigo Sacchi reaped glorious rewards as the San Siro reverberated to the excitement generated by a new era of excellence.

Diego Maradona's 1987 'double-winners' Napoli were pipped to the Italian Championship in 1988. And twelve months later, the Dutch duo steered Milan to an exhilarating 4–0 victory against Steaua Bucharest in the European Cup Final. Both the Dutch stars scored twice as Milan won the trophy for the third time.

Internazionale, refusing to be outdone by their more celebrated neighbours, managed to steal some of Milan's thunder by crowning themselves Italian champions, for the thirteenth time, just four days after Gullit had mesmerised the Rumanian army team in Barcelona.

Milan had become the centre of footballing fashion. And the two sides were to emphasise their supremacy by competing for the European Cup in 1989–90— the perfect *hors d'oeuvre* for the feast of talent on show at the end of the season.

In keeping with the city's rekindled spirit and prestige, the San Siro is being reconstructed to accommodate a new top tier in time for the World Cup Finals. That would increase its all-seated capacity to 90,000 and the San Siro is an object lesson in planning and comfort for modern stadium architects.

Ironically, both clubs looked to the past in their pursuit of excellence. While Gullit, Van Basten and Frank Rijkaard fired Milan's European success, Inter sought championship inspiration from the West German pair Lothar Matthaus and Andreas Brehme.

It was a throwback to the beginning of the century, when both clubs were founded on 'foreign legion' influence. Milan, formed in 1899 by a group of English residents, were the city's forerunners, winning the fledgling Italian Championship three times with a combination of Scots, English and Swiss.

A split in their ranks in 1908 gave birth to Inter, who signed up dissatisfied members of Milan. An intense, sometimes hostile rivalry has existed between the two clubs ever since.

Just to emphasise the benefit of drawing foreign players from a single country, Inter coach Giovanni Trapattoni acquired the services of a third West German, Jurgen Klinsmann, for whom he paid 1989 UEFA Cup finalists VfB Stuttgart £1.3 million, before the start of his club's title defence in 1989–90.

Indeed, the success of Klinsmann's West German team-mates Matthaus and Brehme, who were signed from Bayern Munich in 1988 for £2.5 million and £650,000 respectively, had helped to spare Trapattoni from the wrath of Inter's president, Ernesto Pellegrini.

The adulation and praise bestowed on Milan's 1988 title-winning side greatly irritated the Inter president, for whom heavy spending had not paid off since

SIX
FEET
TALL

UP in the air leap the most formidable trio in Italian football—the Dutch internationals Marco Van Basten, Frank Rijkaard and Ruud Gullit. They brought 1989 glory to Milan in a sweeping 4–0 triumph over Steaua Bucharest in the European Cup Final.

10

succeeding Ivanoe Fraizzoli in 1985. Fortunately for Trapattoni, formerly with Juventus, the contribution of Matthaus and Brehme proved decisive as they guided Inter to their first championship in nine years with four games to spare.

The Inter coach had suffered, just like his immediate predecessors from the ghost of one Helenio Herrera, whose achievements as coach in the mid-1960s catapulted him to legendary status. Inter's awesome defensive steel was the platform from which Herrera launched victories in the European Cup and World Club championships. They won both titles twice, in 1964 and 1965.

Despite their success, Inter have never matched the acclaim and recognition enjoyed by Milan outside the Italian Peninsular. To some extent that was understandable in season 1988–89. The flamboyance of Gullit, Van Basten and Rijkaard contrasted sharply with the industrious reputation that Inter's Brehme and Matthaus carved out for themselves.

Trapattoni, though, had no cause to rue Milan's domination of the entertainment stakes. The impact of his West German imports had removed the stigma created by Inter's embarrassing transfer dealings in the past. The club had

MARCO Van Basten and Ruud Gullit hold high the European Cup which AC Milan will defend against Inter Milan in 1990.

wasted millions on a succession of foreigners, who spent more time testing the ability of their own therapists than those of their opponents. The legacy of injury-prone stars Hansi Muller, Ludo Coeck and Karl-Heinz Rummenigge was that Matthaus and Brehme underwent close scrutiny in their first season.

But their resolution, if not their flair, won over the sceptics, thus enabling Trapattoni to sign the blond, bustling Klinsmann. Trapattoni hoped his arrival as replacement for Ramon Diaz, Argentina's unfulfilled boy-wonder, would add a touch of dash to Inter resilience.

By contrast, Milan's appeal has never been in doubt. Sacchi, appointed in 1987 after several seasons as second division Parma's coach, places more emphasis on attacking football than Trapattoni—not too surprising in view of the wealth of talent at his disposal. Their annihilation of Steaua in the 1989 European Cup Final had critics comparing Milan's performance to Real Madrid's 7–3 European Cup Final defeat of Eintracht Frankfurt in 1960.

Ironically, Milan's 5–0 win against Real in the semi-finals of the competition provided evidence, if needed, of soccer's shifting power base. Milan had replaced bludgeoning Brits Blissett, Hateley and Jordan with Gullit, Van Basten and Rijkaard. A new golden era had begun.

Football, Milan-style, is as near to pageantry as the sport could be. The famous red-and-black shirts evoke memories of great teams of the past, an age when the 'beautiful' football that Milan practise was commonplace.

Milan's 'pressing' tactics, pushing forward to stop the opposition playing, is far from negative. Unlike 'pressing' in Britain, a euphemism for the offside trap, Milan push up to create a launching pad for uninhibited attack. Franco

RUMANIANS remain in close touch with the menacing Van Basten in the European Cup thriller with Steaua Bucharest.

Baresi, the club's inspiring captain and polished central defender, is the catalyst of moves which are as breathtaking as they are sweeping.

Baresi, the club's inspiring captain and polished central defender, is the catalyst of moves which are as breathtaking as they are sweeping.

Class oozes throughout the team. Baresi and his full-backs, Tassotti and Maldini, control and pass the ball better than many forwards. Colombo and Donadoni would grace any midfield, not to mention the much-publicised talents of Gullit, Van Basten and Rijkaard.

Their appeal enticed more than 80,000 fans, the biggest migration of supporters in the history of football, to travel to Barcelona for the 1989 European Cup Final. And their passion is undiluted.

'They are incredible,' says Gullit. 'Milan street life is full of gaiety. People are always wanting to shake my hand. It makes me feel like the Pied Piper.'

Gullit also says that football is a religion for Italians. Unfortunately, a few of them use the game as an outlet for aggression. Adulation of Gullit and his team-mates has provoked hatred from Milan's rivals. It is the same old story and therein lies the one blemish on this great footballing city.

In June, 1989, a nineteen-year-old Roma fan was murdered in a clash with so-called Milan supporters before the sides met in the San Siro. Earlier in the season, an Ascoli fan had been murdered during a match against Inter. In 1987–88, Roma's goalkeeper Franco Tancredi suffered a heart attack on the pitch after being felled by two thunderflashes thrown by Milan fans at the San Siro. Only prompt resuscitation saved his life.

It is a disturbing catalogue of violence and crime. And it would be a crying shame if the wart of hooliganism disfigures the acceptable face of football being proffered by the city of Milan.

RUUD Gullit on the rampage, looking for another goal that would have completed his hat-trick in Milan's 4–0 epic win.

Beware of the Bull!

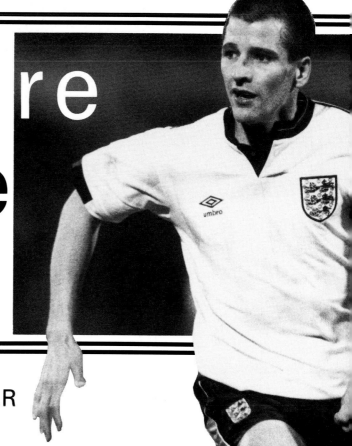

By BRENDAN GALLAGHER
(Sunday Telegraph)

GOALSCORING phenomenon Steve Bull provides living proof that a positive attitude can turn depressing failure into stunning success.

The Wolves and England player was advised by an orthopaedic surgeon to retire from football at the age of sixteen, after a delicate knee operation to repair damaged ligaments and remove floating bone from the joint. Undeterred, he fought back to full fitness and after scoring many goals for his hometown side Tipton Town, he signed professional forms for West Bromwich Albion.

Ron Saunders, a hard man by any criteria, was in charge at The Hawthorns, and although Bull scored regularly for the reserves and three goals in seven first-team appearances, Saunders was not impressed. 'You'll never make it. Your first touch will always let you down,' was his parting message when Bull was transferred to struggling Wolves in the Fourth Division.

For the second time Bull battled to rescue his career—and his subsequent goalscoring pyrotechnics can be explained largely by his determination to prove everybody wrong. In his first season with Wolves he totalled eighteen goals in thirty-three League and Cup games, a strike rate which gave warning of what was to come.

Bull led Wolves to the 1987–88 Division Four championship with thirty-four goals in forty-four matches. He had a further eighteen goals in cup competitions

STEVE Bull (above) looks sharp and ready for action, wearing his England Under-21 shirt against Albania in April 1989.

to end the season with a remarkable total of fifty-two goals in all matches. It was the first time a Football League player had scored fifty in a season since Terry Bly performed the feat with Peterborough in the 1960–61 season.

The following season, Bull continued in prolific goalscoring form. Exercising his exceptional strength and pace, he scored thirty-five League goals, eleven cup goals and four goals in eight appearances for England at various levels.

He reached his League century of goals by scoring a hat-trick against Bristol City in January, 1989, only his 126th League appearance—although, strange to relate, this is not a Wolves record. Dennis Westcott reached his century either side of the War in just 106 games.

Bull's much-vaunted partnership with Andy Mutch was instrumental in Wolves taking the Third Division Championship, and such was his impact that the England manager, Bobby Robson, started taking a serious interest in him.

After three goals in five appearances for the England Under-21 and 'B' sides, Bull became the first Third Division player since Peter Taylor, in 1976, to play for the full England side when he appeared as substitute in the clash against Scotland at Hampden Park. Typically, he marked the occasion with a cracking goal and generally created havoc in the Scottish defence with his forceful and devastatingly direct style.

His club captain, Ally Robertson, speaks enthusiastically about Bull's instinct near goal. 'Soccer hasn't seen the likes of Steve Bull before. He's completely different from any other player I have known,' says the tough Scottish defender.

'His progress over the last two years has been amazing and he can only get better. For one thing he is still learning his trade. For another he still wants to learn. Some lads, with only a fraction of the success he has enjoyed, would have stopped listening long ago.

'One of his secrets is that he never stops looking for goals. Even at the end of a hard, gruelling game, if there's a chance of another strike in the dying seconds he'll go for it. I hope he never loses that attitude and somehow I don't think he will. Just as he won't ever change from being a down-to-earth lad from the Black Country.'

ABOVE The grounded Bull is congratulated by team-mates Neil Webb and Paul Gascoigne after scoring England's second goal against Scotland in the Rous Cup.

OPPOSITE Steve Bull in splendid action, this time wearing promotion-winning Wolves' shirt. And INSET is Ron Saunders, who once told Bull: 'You'll never make it.'

BIG JACK and his JOLLY GREEN GIANTS

THE so-called 'luck of the Irish' has nothing to do with the success of the Republic of Ireland side since Jack Charlton became their manager—yet suddenly it is among the most feared in Europe. Charlton has forged a team which, at worst, is tenacious and difficult to beat and, at its best, is capable of usurping the world's footballing hierarchy with its confident and direct approach.

There has long been a fervent football following in Ireland, but the 49,000 spectators who roared the national side to a 2–0 victory over Hungary in the

By DES KELLY (News of the World)

World Cup qualifier in June, 1989, lay passionate testimony to a new dimension in Irish football . . . BELIEF.

Ireland now realises it can have an impact on world soccer. So does Jack Charlton, albeit more cautiously, when he says: 'We have had tremendous support in our World Cup campaign, with full houses each time. The trouble now is that people expect us to produce a result every time we play. I've had to damp them down a little and say: "Take it easy, the celebrations can start after we win."'

Ireland marked their arrival on the international soccer scene by reaching the last eight of the 1988 European Championships. It was a feat that astonished many, but Ireland shrugged off their underdog tag, beating England 1–0, drawing 1–1 with the runners-up USSR and losing only 0–1 to the eventual champions Holland. The Irish had narrowly missed out from the group that produced both finalists, and the Dutch goal that ended their hopes was, to say the least, questionable.

From the quiet surroundings of his Northumberland home, Charlton was

GARY Lineker is the smiler here, but his opponent Mick McCarthy was the happier man after Eire had beaten England 1–0 in the European Championship.

able to assess his team's achievements, while keeping one eye on the televised Test match cricket: 'We proved that we were able to compete with the best against the Soviet Union. We could have beaten them by two or three goals. We were unlucky against a very good Holland side, but I still think we deserved to get something out of that game, too.'

Charlton was given a reception reserved for conquering heroes on his return. The jet 'plane that flew him back to the Republic was renamed 'St Jack' and Prime Minister Charles Haughey made him an honorary Irishman for taking the side so far in the competition. Thousands upon thousands lined the Dublin streets to greet the team's open-top bus, a welcome that amazed an emotional Charlton. 'It makes you wonder what would have happened if we'd won,' he said as he gazed out at the sea of green, white and gold flags.

On reflection, Charlton rues the loss of key players who may have guided the Irish to greater glory. He says: 'Looking back, I often wonder what would have happened if we had not lost Liam Brady and Mark Lawrenson in the run-up to the Championship. We had to readjust our final plans and that was very difficult to cope with.'

But cope they did and even the Football Association of Ireland (FAI) was taken aback by the success. Because their chances of qualification for the European Championships were regarded as remote, no proper pay bonus scheme for the players was worked out. Ireland's leading players earned around £12,000, in contrast to the England team who took home three times this amount despite losing all three games. There will be no such problems for the World Cup Finals—the FAI made £1 million from the Championships and they are expected to make £2 million if they reach Italy in 1990.

Money matters notwithstanding, Big Jack himself has been depicted as something of a pirate. He lists hunting and shooting as his other pastimes and he has often been accused of plundering from England many promising players with distant Irish ancestry.

Liverpool striker John Aldridge 'qualified' thanks to an Irish grandmother. He embarked on his international career after receiving a call from Charlton telling him to take his family tree to the Irish Football Association. Aldridge's Merseyside teammate, Ray Houghton, is another of Jack's acquisitions, regardless of the fact that he was born in Glasgow. Asked how he could select so many players brandishing English and Scottish accents, Charlton replied: 'Ah, but they *feel* Irish.'

He explains: 'Football is not the number one sport in Ireland and I doubt that there will ever be a day when they can choose from home talent, at least not in the forseeable future. The way ahead depends on a good crop of youngsters playing in England and on the Continent.'

Charlton is gradually introducing new players into the side, but hopes to keep the core of the team together until after the next World Cup. 'We are turning up players like Norwich City's Andy Townsend, who played well against Hungary, and there are one or two others on the fringe at the moment.

'After the World Cup I will be bringing in some new faces and one or two

OPPOSITE, on the left Ray Houghton and right Kevin Moran, two stalwarts of Jack Charlton's team of Irish giantkillers.

ONE FOR THE POT

NAKED and unashamed is the gritty Eire centre-half Mick McCarthy, his arm raised in salute as Jack Charlton's team continue to shock the big nations of world soccer.

of the regular side will be playing less. But it is very difficult to plan for the long term in international football; often you have to make the most of whoever turns up on the day.

'I don't like to pick out individuals—no manager does—but I think Ronnie Whelan, Kevin Moran, Mick McCarthy, Ray Houghton and Tony Cascarino have really put themselves about. And Paul McGrath has been outstanding in all his international appearances.'

Charlton, an ex-guardsman, coalminer, a proud holder of the OBE and a World Cup-winning Englishman, has had no qualms about throwing himself behind the Republican cause. 'There was a time when I badly wanted to be the England manager,' he confesses, but despite this longing and his firm English roots, there can be no doubting where Charlton's loyalty lies now. 'My heart is 100 per cent with the Republic,' he says.

The marriage between manager and country got off to a stormy start. The FAI appointed Charlton amid confusion and controversy. Former Irish manager (and Charlton's Leeds team-mate) John Giles was discarded and former Liverpool boss Bob Paisley was out-voted, leaving Charlton as the surprise choice. He was by no means welcomed with open arms by everyone. 'Go home Union Jack' declared one banner at Charlton's first match in charge, but those banners have long since been discarded and the Irish have taken him to their hearts.

The job is officially billed as part-time, but to Charlton that simply means

TRICKY moment here for Liverpool skipper Ronnie Whelan, another of the trusty Charlton squad when he's not winning medals at Anfield.

that he is freed from the daily administration of club matters and has more time to concentrate on his team. 'I plan the hotels and travel arrangements; everything happens through me. I decide where we'll train and get in touch with the lads myself. I don't like it when things happen that I don't know about,' he says.

To say that he is unconventional would be something of an understatement. Charlton arrived at a Press conference to announce his team to face Rumania in 1988 with the names scribbled on the back of a cigarette packet. Midway through his team announcement, Charlton found that he couldn't make out one of the names written on the box and had to be prompted by a Press man. Then he mistakenly referred to Rumania as Bulgaria.

Yet far from sapping confidence in his abilities, it is this rough and ready quality which has done much to endear Charlton to the football public.

On a trip to London with Leeds United, Charlton is said to have ordered melon before his soup at an exclusive restaurant. He was then quietly informed by a waiter that 'nobody eats melon before soup.' He promptly got up, advised them how they should dispose of their meal and walked out.

Charlton favours the simple recipe, the simple life and the simple approach to football. He reduces the most involved tactical briefings to straightforward, no-nonsense language. And the pattern of play he has established for the Republic is simplicity itself. The players have been instructed to run farther, run harder, dwell less on the ball and put opponents under pressure by attacking them at pace.

'I came to a conscious decision after the World Cup in Mexico about the way I wanted the side to play,' he said. 'I thought that everyone out there played exactly the same sort of football. They sat back and allowed the other side space and built the move up slowly from the back. They didn't make a challenge for the ball until it reached the last third of the field.

'But I have tried to pin down a pattern of play which is simple to follow. I tell the lads to close them down early, hit the ball past the full-backs and get behind the defence. Now I'm beginning to see more national sides adopt that approach. The Irish lads have the ability to compete and I'd back them against any team in the world when they do that.'

Charlton himself has competed at every level. He made 770 appearances for Leeds United, scoring ninety-five goals in that time. He has First and Second Division Championship medals, FA Cup, League Cup and Fairs Cup winners' medals, and was capped thirty-five times by England, scoring on six occasions. And, most important of all, he has a 1966 World Cup winners' medal.

Before the Irish job, he managed Middlesbrough, Sheffield Wednesday and Newcastle United, winning the Second Division Championship in 1973–74 with Middlesbrough. So there can be no doubting Charlton's credentials.

'At the moment I can do no wrong and everyone in Ireland loves me—that is because the team is doing so well. The real test will come when a few results go against us,' he says, 'although I can't see that happening in the near future . . .'

SEASON 1988–89 was one of endless successes for Eire 'cap' Tony Cascarino as he totted up the goals for Millwall.

WILKINS

(Eighty-four internationals for England)

IS PICK OF THE SCOTS

RAY WILKINS' selection as the 'Premier Division's skill player for 1988–89' simply confirmed suspicions that had played on his mind since November, 1987, when he joined Rangers from Paris St. Germain.

Wilkins, so often the butt of cruel jibes in England for supposedly being too negative in his technique, is not half as 'square' north of the Border according to Scottish fans. 'Without doubt, I am more respected by people in Scotland than I ever was in England,' says the London-born midfielder, who was thirty-three on September 14, 1989.

Wilkins' assertion that he has not changed his style to fit into the rough-and-tumble environment of Scottish football adds further credence to a remarkable tale. It is one of resilience and flair—qualities not associated with Wilkins before he was almost hounded out of English football to join Italian giants Milan for £1.5 million in 1984.

At Manchester United, he became accustomed to groans rumbling from the terraces whenever his trademark, a nonchalant sideways pass, left his boot. His critics felt it was a betrayal of the attacking principles and entertainment which are said to inspire Manchester United, whose colours Wilkins wore between 1979 and 1984.

However, even in the darkest hours of unpopularity, the former England captain remained dignified and refused to stoop to the levels of his detractors. 'The important thing in any walk of life is to have confidence in your own ability,' he says. 'If you don't, then nobody else will.

'I only have to look at some of the managers who have played me (*Ron Greenwood, Dave Sexton, Ron Atkinson, Bobby Robson and Graeme Souness*) and I know they are better judges than the people who criticised me,' says Wilkins.

Although it would be a major surprise if he represented his country again, the eighty-four caps he won for England stand testimony to his prowess. Meanwhile, his reputation as a survivor has been enhanced at Ibrox.

He made his Football League debut for Chelsea as long ago as 1973, but not even experience gained in the intervening period could prepare him for the culture shock he confronted in Scotland. As he says: 'No question about it, this is the fastest and most physical football I have ever played.

'In my first match against Hearts, I honestly thought I wouldn't be able to make a go of it. After about ten or fifteen minutes, I remember asking Graham Roberts when the final whistle was going.'

The new two-year contract that Rangers' manager Graeme Souness put before Wilkins in the 1989 close season is indicative of the impact he made after that testing start. Wilkins, who seems to have been oozing class and confidence for an eternity, was as inspirational as any of his team-mates in Rangers' march to a League Championship and Skol Cup double in the 1988–89 season.

Just how influential was made abundantly clear to Souness in that season's Scottish Cup Final, when Wilkins' absence through injury undermined his sides's challenge against Glasgow rivals Celtic. What made a 1–0 defeat more galling was the fact that it denied Rangers a fantastic treble.

That Wilkins adapted to the hurly-burly of Scottish football, after a comparatively pedestrian three-year spell on the Continent with Milan and Paris St. Germain, illustrates his immense talent. In doing so, he answered his critics in the manner he knows best—on the field.

The ability to pick locks in opposing defences, no matter how physically taxing the environment, with such touch and vision makes Wilkins a true exponent of the finer arts and crafts.

'The important thing in any walk of life is to have confidence in your own ability . . .'

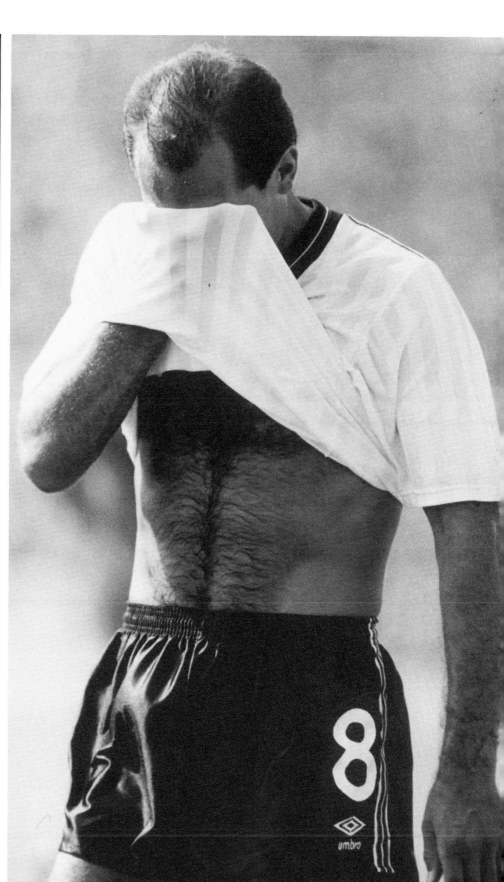

THESE were sad-happy
moments for Ray Wilkins.
Happy in his cool-it mood for
Rangers . . . sad on one of his
black-mark occasions for
England after being sent off
in the World Cup match with
Morocco.

BRAZILIAN star Romario, in menacing mood here for Brazil, was a star of the Eindhoven championship hat-trick win.

TWO 'FIRSTS' FOR BRAZILIAN ACES

By JOHN PRICE (The People)

BRAZIL! The mere mention of the country is enough to evoke memories of spectacular goals, magical skills and marvellous technique. Of great players. Of Pelé and Didi, Rivelino and Tostao. Socrates and Zico. Quite simply, Brazil means football at its best.

Nowhere was that claim more perfectly illustrated in the 1988–89 season than in the European football hotbeds of Naples and Eindhoven where two of the modern-day generation of Brazilian stars led their respective clubs to notable 'firsts'.

The goals of Antonio Oliveira Filho, better known simply as Careca, carried Napoli to their first European trophy, the UEFA Cup; Romario de Souza Faria topped PSV Eindhoven's scoring charts as the club won the Dutch League title for the third successive time—a feat previously achieved only by Ajax between 1966 and 1968.

The similarities between both men are numerous. Each is short and compact, with subtle touch and powerful shot, with total self-confidence and an insatiable appetite for goals.

But perhaps the greatest asset is that which no amount of training can produce . . . INSTINCT. Both possess the uncanny ability of being in the right place at the right time to snap up any half-chances, as well as having enough skill to create openings of their own.

The emergence of Careca as the hero of Napoli's historic UEFA Cup win—he finished as the competition's joint top scorer with six goals alongside Gutschow of Dynamo Dresden—owed much to his partnership with Argentinian Diego Maradona. Their importance to Napoli was underlined in the final against VfB Stuttgart.

Trailing at home in the first leg to a shock opening German strike, the Maradona-Careca combination conjured a goal apiece in a stirring second-half revival to secure a 2–1 win. Then, in the return leg, the deadly South American double act struck again, playing a leading part in goals for team-mates Alemao and Ferrara before Maradona set up Careca for what proved to be the decisive goal in a 5–4 aggregate victory.

Not that it has been all plain sailing between them. Following his £3 million transfer from Sao Paulo in June, 1987, Careca walked into a public row between the Napoli management and Maradona, who wanted his younger brother Hugo to join him as the club's second overseas player rather than the Brazilian.

However, out of the initial uneasiness caused by the little Argentinian's tantrum came mutual respect between the two as their partnership began to bear fruit.

Maradona, with fifteen goals, and Careca, thirteen, topped the Serie A scoring charts in 1987–88; but for all their impressive scoring exploits, Napoli had to settle for second place behind the Gullit-Van Basten inspired Milan who pipped them for the title in the final weeks.

Careca made amends for that disappointment a year later with his leading role in the club's UEFA Cup success, thus ensuring honorary status for himself among the Neopolitan faithful.

The diminutive Romario became the hottest property in world football following his explosive exploits in the Olympic Games in Seoul. He was the competition's top scorer with seven goals, including a hat-trick against Australia, as Brazil finished as runners-up to the Russians.

The twenty-three-year-old striker could have had his pick of any number of big Continental clubs, among them Benfica, Atletico Madrid and Torino, but he opted for the then European champions PSV Eindhoven, who offered him a massive financial package that even the giants of Italy and Spain could not match.

His £3.2 million transfer from Vasco de Gama in October, 1988 (a record fee for a Brazilian) put him into the film stars' wage bracket, earning £600,000 a year and massive bonuses. He lives in a sumptuous apartment, drives a Porsche and sends his children to private school.

Romario began to pay off his massive fee immediately, scoring on his debut for the club, and he finished as the Dutch League's top marksman with nineteen goals—a remarkable feat in that he entered the Dutch season nearly six weeks late because of his involvement in Seoul.

Although Eindhoven lost their grip on the European Cup—they were beaten by Real Madrid in the quarter-finals—Romario's goals ensured recompense in the form of a domestic Cup-League double success.

Whatever Careca and Romario achieve at club level, both realise they will ultimately be judged in Brazil's hall of fame by their achievements at the highest level, namely the World Cup. Careca proved himself worthy of the game's premier stage in the 1986 Mexico Finals, scoring five goals, a feat bettered only by Gary Lineker's six for England.

However, Brazil's hopes of World Cup glory were shattered in the quarter-finals by France, who recovered from Careca's brilliant first-half goal to win the match in a dramatic penalty shoot-out.

Romario, who made his debut for Brazil on the 1988 tour to Australia, had yet to be tested at the highest international level, but he showed enough class in the Olympic Games to suggest he could more than hold his own if called upon.

Indeed, if Brazil can continue the trend of having qualified for the final stages of every World Cup into the nineties, then Careca and Romario may yet emulate Pelé, Didi and Tostao and claim a lasting place in Brazilian folklore.

HERE'S a double take of another
brilliant Brazilian seeking cash and
glory on the European circuit. It's
Careca, the man from Mars—
otherwise Napoli, whom he helped
to their UEFA Cup triumph against
Stuttgart.

World Cup 199(

★ ★ ★ ★ ★ ★ ★ ★

KEIR RADNEDG

(Editor of 'World Soccer')

SETS THE SCENE

★ ★ ★ ★ ★ ★ ★ ★

Twenty-six billior

ITALIANS knew as far back as 1984 that their beloved national team, the Azzurri (*The Blues*), would not need to brave the qualifying fire on their way to the finals of 1990.

December that year was the point in the calendar at which FIFA's all powerful executive committee decided that Italy should become the first European nation allowed the honour of hosting the World Cup Finals twice.

Italy were the first-ever European hosts, back in 1934. A team inspired by legendary inside-forward Giuseppe Meazza and iron man centre-half Luisito Monti also finished up as winners, beating Czechoslovakia 2–1 in the Final in Rome.

Can history repeat itself? The omens look good. Hosts have won five of

.. Italy beckons

will watch Finals

the thirteen World Cups staged since the inaugural kick-off back in Uruguay in 1930. And in 1990, as in 1934, Rome will lay out a fanatical red carpet for the Final. Only the size of the audience will have changed.

In 1934, a total of 395,000 fans were the 'only' witnesses to soccer's greatest event. This time, courtesy of television, the twenty-four competing finalists play not only for the World Cup, but for a worldwide audience of twenty-six billion!

It is for all these eyes that multinational corporations, skilfully set in place by FIFA's Swiss-based commercial agents, ISL Marketing, will pay millions of pounds to advertise their wares. Just as international big business intends using the World Cup to 'sell' their videos, films, soft drinks and photocopiers,

ABOVE Napoli Stadium, one of the venues for the World Cup, is under close scrutiny here from a police helicopter.

so Italy's own business and political leaders hope to use the World Cup to 'sell' their country in the tourist markets of the world.

This is a country with a rare capacity to delight and astonish the visitor. The sights are apparently infinite. From Rome, with the Coliseum and Spanish Steps, to Milan with a musical authority rooted at La Scala, to Turin with its colonnaded sophistication, to Florence with its artistic treasures . . . all this is the tip of an Italy awaiting rediscovery via a few football matches.

Organising this gigantic circus is no easy matter. For instance, the head of the Spanish organising committee in 1982, Raimundo Saporta, came to the brink of a nervous breakdown because of the problems and the pressure. And this was a man who helped build in Real Madrid one of the world's most powerful clubs!

Heading up the *Italia 90* organisation is a man named Luca di Montezemolo. His name may mean nothing to those whose passion for sport begins and ends with football players. But Montezemolo is in a different league. A forty-one-year-old lawyer, Montezemolo happens to be one of the blue-eyed protégés of the multi-millionaire owner of the FIAT motor giant, Gianni Agnelli.

It was Agnelli who first entrusted the young Montezemolo with a senior

management role within the Ferrari motor-racing 'stable.' Likewise, there is no doubt the Agnelli influence was again at work backing Montezemolo to become director-general of the Italian World Cup organising committee.

Montezemolo soon proved a thorough leader, demanding the freedom to attend the 1986 World Cup Finals in Mexico and wandering in and out of stadia, studying facilities and potential. From that trip came the decisions to demand structural redevelopment in all of the World Cup venues.

Montezemolo's advisers warned him that such work could cost more than £100 million and immediately sought financial support from the government. It was not his fault that a government crisis meant financial clearance arrived only eighteen months before the Finals are due to begin.

Whether that is long enough for stadia controllers in Naples, Rome and Turin to organise for 1990 is in some doubt. Whether the Stadio Olimpico in Rome will be covered is one unknown factor. Another concerns the new stadium being built in Turin and whether that will be ready in time. Otherwise Turin, one of Italy's great soccer cities, could be wiped out of the programme altogether.

Italy's soccer fans, however, have faith. The first batch of tickets have long since been put on sale in Italy—and sold out in two days.

The *tifosi* obviously believe all problems to be minor. After all, if Argentina, Spain and Mexico could stage World Cups despite the assorted threats of urban terrorism, uncontrollable political in-fighting and an earthquake, there seems no reason to doubt Italy's potential. Of course, the international media may spread a few panic stories along the way. But Montezemolo is coolly confident he can still hit most of his important deadlines.

When it comes to panic talk, few items could have been so far off target

HERE'S a ground-level shot of Sampdoria's ground, which will be closed for vital works for half the season leading up to the World Cup.

as the stories that FIFA had told the Italians their pitches were too big. The truth of that is that FIFA insists that all pitches at the Finals should be the same dimensions. Therefore, since Udine has the smallest pitch of the twelve venues, the grand stadia of Milan, Rome and the rest have to cut down to the smallest common denominator—that is, 105 metres by 68 metres.

Already some suspicious minds are suggesting that this is a ploy to help the Italians, since smaller pitches make *catenaccio* that much easier to operate!

Vujadin Boskov, coach to Sampdoria, blames it all on Spain's World Cup hosting of 1982. He says: 'The 105 by 68 dimensions were those of Sarria in Barcelona, of Malaga and of Seville. So the regulations were amended to tighten all the other Spanish pitches down to those. Personally I regret it. Big pitches are for great teams, small pitches are for small-minded teams.'

World Cup venue

GROUP A: *Olimpico, Rome (capacity 71,180), Communale, Florence (66,344)*

Sat, June 9	Rome	. . . . v . . . .
Sun, June 10	Florence	. . . . v . . . .
Thu, June 14	Rome	. . . . v . . . .
Fri, June 15	Florence	. . . . v . . . .
Tue, June 19	Rome	. . . . v . . . .
Tue, June 19	Florence	. . . . v . . . .

GROUP B: *Opening Game at Meazza, Milan (83,141). Also San Paolo, Naples (85,102) and Della Vittoria, Bari (40,400)*

Fri, June 8	Milan	. . . . v . . . .
Sat, June 9	Bari	. . . . v . . . .
Wed, June 13	Naples	. . . . v . . . .
Thu, June 14	Bari	. . . . v . . . .
Mon, June 18	Naples	. . . . v . . . .
Mon, June 18	Bari	. . . . v . . . .

GROUP C: *Turin (70,000), Luigi Ferraris, Genoa (54,872)*

Sun, June 10	Turin	. . . . v . . . .
Mon, June 11	Genoa	. . . . v . . . .
Sat, June 16	Turin	. . . . v . . . .
Sat, June 16	Genoa	. . . . v . . . .
Wed, June 20	Turin	. . . . v . . . .
Wed, June 20	Genoa	. . . . v . . . .

Sampdoria are one club directly affected by the World Cup's proximity. For one thing, the Luigi Ferraris stadium they share with neighbours Genoa is closed for half a season while structural work takes place; and Sampdoria will receive nothing by way of financial compensation. Then, Sampdoria also boast the young superstar Gianluca Vialli, on whose wiry, slim shoulders will be placed all of Italy's hopes and dreams.

If Vialli scores the goals Italy demands and the hosts win the World Cup for a record fourth time, then he can look to a £10 million, world record-breaking transfer.

That is a measure of the sort of money available in Italian football. The Agnelli family, who own FIAT and Juventus, have run the club as a personal business toy since the 1920s; Silvio Berlusconi, the television magnate, spent

e draw will be made on December 9 in Rome. Argen-
a, as holders, are expected to be based in Naples, hosts
ly based in Rome.

GROUP D: *Meazza, Milan (83,141), Renato Dell'Ara, Bologna (49,500)*

Sat, June 9	Bologna	.... v ....
Sun, June 10	Milan	.... v ....
Thu, June 14	Bologna	.... v ....
Fri, June 15	Milan	.... v ....
Tue, June 19	Milan	.... v ....
Tue, June 19	Bologna	.... v ....

GROUP E: *Comunale, Verona (42,000), Friuli, Udine (48,847)*

Tue, June 12	Verona	.... v ....
Wed, June 13	Udine	.... v ....
Sun, June 17	Verona	.... v ....
Sun, June 17	Udine	.... v ....
Thu, June 21	Verona	.... v ....
Thu, June 21	Udine	.... v ....

GROUP F: *Sant'Elia, Cagliari (60,000), Della Favorita, Palermo (42,000)*

Mon, June 11	Cagliari	.... v ....
Tue, June 12	Palermo	.... v ....
Sat, June 16	Cagliari	.... v ....
Sun, June 17	Palermo	.... v ....
Thu, June 21	Cagliari	.... v ....
Thu, June 21	Palermo	.... v ....

MORE VENUES ON NEXT TWO PAGES ▶

£20 million turning Milan into European champions (by paying off the club's debts and then securing the finance to sign Dutch greats Ruud Gullit, Marco Van Basten and Frank Rijkaard); Ernesto Pellegrini, president of Italian champions Internazionale, is a pasta millionaire; Sampdoria's Paolo Mantovani made his fortune with an oil tanker fleet after the Six Day War in the Middle East.

These are all important men with financial and political muscle. Yet none, in World Cup terms, ranks as highly as all-powerful FIFA officials such as president Joao Havelange, general secretary Sepp Blatter and FIFA World Cup boss Hermann Neuberger.

This demanding trio have made little secret of their displeasure at the snags which mean Italy will fail to match promises of new roads and improved airport facilities. Montezemolo admits the point, saying: 'Italy has missed a great chance to use the World Cup organisation to advantage.' But he also adds: 'Fortunately, we will at least have twelve modernised stadia, sell-out crowds and great tourist opportunities.'

Responsibility for a successful World Cup is thus transferred to the shoulders of Italian national manager Azeglio Vicini. If Italy win the World Cup for a record-breaking fourth time, all the confusion in the corridors of power will be forgotten.

If not, as Montezemolo surely knows, Vicini will go down . . . and take Montezemolo with him.

World Cup venue

SECOND ROUND

Sat, June 23	Naples	B1 v A3/C3/D3	. . . . v . . . .
Sat, June 23	Bari	A2 v C2	. . . . v . . . .
Sun, June 24	Turin	C1 v A3/B3/F3	. . . . v . . . .
Sun, June 24	Milan	D1 v B3/E3/F3	. . . . v . . . .
Mon, June 25	Rome	A1 v C3/D3/E3	. . . . v . . . .
Mon, June 25	Genoa	F2 v B2	. . . . v . . . .
Tue, June 26	Bologna	F1 v E2	. . . . v . . . .
Tue, June 26	Verona	E1 v D2	. . . . v . . . .

QUARTER FINALS

Sat, June 30	Rome	W/Genoa v W/Rome	. . . . v . . . .
Sat, June 30	Florence	W/Turin v W/Verona	. . . . v . . . .
Sun, July 1	Naples	W/Naples v W/Bologna	. . . . v . . . .
Sun, July 1	Milan	W/Bari v W/Milan	. . . . v . . . .

. . closing stages

SEMI-FINALS

Tue, July 3   Naples   W/Florence v W/Rome   .... v ....

Wed, July 4   Turin   W/Milan v W/Naples   .... v ....

THIRD PLACE MATCH

Sat, July 7   Bari   .... v ....

THE FINAL

Sun, July 8   Rome   .... v ....

LOOKING ahead to the Polish goal, and the World Cup Finals beyond, is Peter Beardsley as he clashes with Poland's Waldemar Matysik in their qualifying game. England won 3–0.

As Peter Shilton was saying to his England skipper Bryan Robson . . .

It must be

PETER SHILTON was asked after he had won his one-hundreth England cap whether he was disappointed that the total wasn't nearer two hundred.

During the managership of Ron Greenwood, Shilton had had to share the goalkeeping duties with Ray Clemence. 'No,' said Shilton, 'I'm glad Ray won those caps. He was a good goalkeeper.'

On the occasion he won his 109th international cap and thus became the most-capped Englishman, Shilton was given the opportunity to lead England on to the pitch for the match against Denmark in Copenhagen, but he declined the offer of his captain, Bryan Robson. It must be business as usual, he insisted.

Both incidents are typical of Peter Shilton. A dedicated, no-nonsense professional who deservedly holds the reputation as one of the safest goalkeepers England has ever had. It is a remarkable achievement for a player who, on the strength of a shot he let slip under his body from Poland's Domarski that effectively cost England a place in the 1974 World Cup Finals, was regarded as unreliable by some people for many years.

Shilton has always had talent. He made his first appearance for England against East Germany at Wembley in November, 1970, when he was only twenty-one years of age, and he has built up his present aura of near invincibility through unceasing hard work.

Ray Clemence is one of Shilton's greatest admirers, saying: 'Even when

By ALASTAIR YEOMANS

SHILTON discusses a knotty problem with England manager Bobby Robson. Obviously something worth shouting about!

ousiness
as usual

everyone else has finished training, Peter stays until he has satisfied himself. He prepares very correctly and thinks about the game very deeply.'

Shilton himself says: 'I only train for an hour and a half each day, but I put so much into it that I don't have much energy left when I'm finished.' The reason he continues to torture his body, after a quarter of a century in the professional game, is simple. 'Any goal that gets past me, for club or country, I treat as a personal disaster,' he says. 'I don't like to be beaten at anything. That's what has kept me working and training hard all these years.'

Shilton, who began his career at the age of sixteen with Leicester City as understudy to Gordon Banks, names three goalkeepers whom he particularly admired: *LEV YASHIN*, the Russian goalkeeper, whose black strip and air of invincibility used to intimidate opposition forwards; *PETER BONETTI* for the way he dealt with crosses and distributed the ball; and *GORDON BANKS* himself, whose positioning was so good that he made even the most difficult save look simple.

Shilton became the regular goalkeeper at Leicester when Banks was trans-

Clough: It would be worth charging to watch him train

ferred to Stoke City and played in his first major final in 1969, when Leicester were beaten 1–0 by Manchester City in the FA Cup.

He played 286 League games for Leicester City and 110 for Stoke City before being transferred to Nottingham Forest for £270,000 in September, 1977. He won a League Championship winners' medal in 1978, European Cup winners' medals in 1979 and 1980, and a League Cup winners' medal in 1979 with Nottingham Forest.

He was reported to have had an occasionally tempestuous relationship with the Forest manager, Brian Clough, but he would never criticise his boss, who in turn held Shilton in the highest regard. 'The lads have been open-mouthed at Shilton in training,' Clough once said. 'It would be worth charging people to watch him.'

After playing a total of 272 games for Nottingham Forest, Shilton moved to Southampton and then Derby County. On April 30, 1988, he played for Derby against Watford at Vicarage Road to break Terry Paine's record of 824 League appearances.

The top players are in no doubt why he has remained at the top. Striker Kerry Dixon, of Chelsea and England, says: 'When a goalkeeper is as good

HAVING won 109 caps for England, it was a little different for Shilton as he received a unique '109' shirt before the match with Denmark in Copenhagen.

as Shilton, he prowls around the goal area like a lion. His presence intimidates forwards. I've never worried about any centre-half as much as I have about him.'

Bob Wilson, the former Arsenal goalkeeper, says: 'His standards are incredibly high and, amazingly, he is still achieving them. His handling is excellent, he dominates his penalty box and his reflexes aren't much slower than when he made his debut. Any youngster wanting to make the grade as a goalkeeper should study the great man.'

In the international arena, Shilton's achievements have been outstanding.

LEFT Gordon Banks in his playing days, for whom Shilton understudied at Leicester. RIGHT Peter (The Cat) Bonetti, another ex-England man now passing on the wise words to Chelsea's young 'keepers.

He still has a great stature and presence – Bobby Robson

He has guarded England's goal under five managers: Sir Alf Ramsey, Joe Mercer (caretaker), Don Revie, Ron Greenwood and Bobby Robson. He had won only thirty-seven England caps up to the age of thirty-two, but collected a further seventy-two in the next seven years. In all those appearances, he kept fifty-eight clean sheets.

Shilton still seeks a winners' medal in a major international championship. He had long set his mind on playing in the World Cup Finals in Italy in 1990, when he will be forty. There is a precedent. Italy's goalkeeper Dino Zoff was forty when he captained them to World Cup success in 1982.

Bobby Robson says: 'There are days when Peter has saved us. He still has a great stature and presence and, for me, he is still our number one. He has never let us down and so how can I ever think about leaving him out?'

UNDERSTUDY to Shilton for so long in the England squad is Chris Woods, seen here in Rangers' goal tipping the ball over the bar after a Celtic raid in the Scottish Cup Final of 1989.

GLENN HYSEN

'In my first game I gave away a penalty in the first minute. I was so ashamed'

By IAN CRUISE (Sunday Mirror)

GLENN HYSEN, Sweden's stylish central defender, is convinced that the 1990 World Cup Finals in Italy will be unlike any football tournament ever staged.

Hysen, who is the lynchpin of Sweden's team at the age of thirty, is well qualified to pass judgment after playing club football for one of the leading Italian sides, Fiorentina. He says: 'The finals will be something special. People in Italy have been talking about the World Cup since the summer of 1988.'

And Hysen said at that time: 'Whenever I went out, they would stop me in the street and all they wanted to talk about was football twenty-four hours a day. If you go to a party all the conversation revolves around football.'

That is one of the biggest differences Hysen has found about football in Italy and Sweden. Though the sport is popular in his home country, it is by no means the be-all and end-all it is in Italy. 'Football is like a religion in Italy. Maybe after the tournament has ended things will die down a little.'

Hysen's background is far removed from the pressure-cooker atmosphere in which he now plays. He grew up in Hisingen, a heavy industrial island in Gothenburg, and as a child he was very close to his father Kurt. He recalls:

'Dad and I played football all the time and he is the one who has done most for me in my career.'

Hysen began his career with a minor Swedish team, Warta, and was transferred to their powerful neighbours, IFK Gothenburg, in 1978. By then he had already won seventeen caps for Sweden at youth level.

In 1979 a new young coach, Sven-Goran Eriksson, arrived at Gothenburg, bringing with him new ideas which met with stiff resistance at first, especially from the Press. But Hysen says: 'The players always believed in him. Apart from my dad, he taught me most of my football skills.'

In return, Eriksson had confidence in Hysen but his Swedish League career did not get off to the best of starts. He says: 'In my first game I gave away a penalty in the first minute. I was so ashamed.'

But things improved and in 1982, when IFK were probably the best-ever Swedish club side, Hysen helped them to win the UEFA Cup. A year later he signed for the Dutch club PSV Eindhoven, but he found it hard to settle in Holland and, eighteen months later, he returned home to Gothenburg.

In 1987 the club again won the UEFA Cup and again Hysen was on the move. Manchester United were keen to sign him but the big-money offer from Fiorentina, and the fact that Eriksson was their coach, was just too good to refuse.

Hysen says: 'The money in Italy is incredible and it's very easy to attract the top players because they know how well paid they will be. The Italian League is certainly the strongest I have played in and that is because clubs can afford to buy the best players in the world.

'The game in Italy is very fast and technical whereas, in Sweden, there is much more emphasis on tactics. The one aspect of the game I did not enjoy in Italy was the way players fake injury when they are not really hurt at all. That just causes unnecessary stoppages and is wrong.'

Although Hysen turned Manchester United down in 1987, he remained keen to test his skills in the Football League. He says: 'I came very close to signing for United then. Everything was agreed with Mr Ferguson and Martin Edwards, the chairman, but then Fiorentina came along with a much better offer.

'I liked it in Italy but, for me and a lot of other Swedes, English football is something special, having grown up watching English games on television every Saturday. There are a lot of good clubs in England and I am very happy to have signed for one of the greatest in Liverpool.'

Hysen would welcome a return of English clubs to European competition. He says: 'It is time they were allowed back, even if they have to leave their fans behind. We need variety in Europe, so we need English clubs to provide a contrast from the way Italian and Spanish clubs play.

'It is not only the English fans who cause trouble. There are fights during and after games in Italy, and in West Germany during the 1988 European Championships the Dutch and the Germans were bad as well.'

Hysen's approach to the game should certainly be a welcome boost to English football.

Scapegoat Mark is back on top

THERE can be no greater honour than to be voted the best in your profession by your peers. Manchester United's powerful striker Mark Hughes had that honour bestowed on him when the Professional Footballers' Association chose him as their Player of the Year for 1989.

It was a choice that surprised many, for the soccer pundits argued that United's poor showing in 1988–89 hardly merited the recognition of one of its stars. But the pro's begged to differ and elected Hughes for his devastating return to form following a harrowing two years abroad.

Hughes suffered a crisis in confidence when he left United for Barcelona in May, 1986. Terry Venables, then manager of the Spanish giants, signed the Welsh international for £2.3 million to partner Gary Lineker in a potentially electrifying striking partnership.

But he was not successful in the Catalan capital and the intensity of the Spanish media spotlight fell mercilessly on every missed chance. Many players may consider they are not given a fair chance at Barcelona and four goals in

GLAMOUR days for Mark Hughes, seen above with Gary Lineker before kick-off in the vast Nou Camp Stadium of Barcelona.

New lease of life . . .

TIMES were hard at Barcelona, but it was a new, inspired Mark Hughes back at Old Trafford in his favourite red shirt.

seven months was not enough to keep the Press and the public at bay, as Hughes himself says:

'Quite simply, I didn't get enough goals at Barcelona. I was bought as a striker and, because I wasn't scoring regularly, people thought I wasn't doing my job. I was under a lot of pressure which increased every game I didn't get a goal. I began snatching at the opportunities that came my way and I was caught in a vicious circle.'

Barcelona failed to overhaul rivals Real Madrid in the race for the Spanish title and Hughes increasingly became a scapegoat. A surprise UEFA Cup quarter-final defeat at the hands of Dundee United in the once impregnable Nou Camp Stadium proved the final straw and Hughes found himself out of favour.

His football future looked to have reached a deadlock. After Venables' departure, Barcelona took less and less interest in their troubled striker and Hughes was only released from his state of limbo when the West German club Bayern Munich took him on loan.

'It certainly gave me the chance to get my career back on an even keel,' he said. 'It got to the stage where I was not even playing at Barcelona—just training—which was no use whatsoever.'

Even so, the Munich management were apparently not too impressed by what they saw on the training pitch in the first weeks.

Hughes says: 'It's always been the same story . . . I'm lousy on the training pitch. If I am not physically involved in the game, I am not the same player. I am not going to be stupid, but if someone wants to fight I'll take him on.

'That means I have to hold back because I would be hurting everybody if I played my normal game. And that's not too clever when you're putting team-mates in the casualty room.'

But he is a firm believer in dishing out as much treatment as he receives on the football field—and he gets plenty. 'Every game I come off the pitch, I can hardly move for the bangs and the bumps, but I am heavily built and I recover quickly. Even so, I have played with strains because I didn't want to lose my place.'

Bayern were happy enough with Hughes' performances in competitive matches and looked like holding on to the talented striker when his loan spell came to an end, but Manchester United took the burly Welshman back to Old Trafford for £1.5 million in June, 1988.

On his return to Old Trafford, Hughes found a new lease of life. His game showed a great improvement. The experience of man-to-man marking in the Spanish League improved his ability to turn his opponents and find more space amid the more positional defences of English football.

Hughes was at last fulfilling the potential he had displayed from an early age, when he had so impressed the Manchester United scouts while playing for Ruabon, on the outskirts of Wrexham, that he began receiving Christmas cards from the club as a twelve-year-old.

He went to Old Trafford as an apprentice three years later, playing in midfield. But after four months at United, when he was struggling to make the grade, United's team coach Syd Owen said he thought a switch to a front position would help—and he hasn't looked back. Hughes finished as top scorer for the youth team in 1981–82 and spent two seasons with the Central League side before scoring on his first-team debut.

Arthur Graham was injured before a Milk Cup tie against Oxford United and Hughes was thrown into the side when he hadn't even expected to be substitute. He scored with a header and, still conscious that he was the 'new boy', he hardly dared celebrate what was the most significant goal of his life. He raised his hand, just for a second, in an embarrassed wave.

Despite scoring again on his international debut for Wales in their 1–0 victory over England at Wrexham in 1984, Hughes faced the start of the 1984–85 season not only with Frank Stapleton and Norman Whiteside as United's established strikers, but also the competition of the new £600,000 signing Alan Brazil. But there was no stopping the rising star and he was crowned United's Player of the Year at the end of that season.

'There was a place up for grabs because Frank Stapleton was out,' said Hughes. 'So I thought if I had a good pre-season run there was a chance. Luckily I was able to score a few goals so I was in. Then, thankfully, I steered clear of injury because it's not so easy to get back in that team when you have to drop out.

'My fitness was also important. The speed of First Division football is a shock to the system at first, but once I had got the physical side of the game right the rest of it followed on.'

There can be no doubting his excellent all-round quality. Strength, flair, close control, aggression, pace and heading ability all combine to make him one of the most feared strikers in the Football League. But despite all of this, Hughes remains a shy and unassuming character and this may have prompted last year's PFA award.

'I'm a quiet person off the field. I don't go round shouting my mouth off because it's not in my nature,' he says. 'But when I get on the pitch, the noise of the crowd gets my adrenalin pumping. I love it!'

At Manchester United, manager Alex Ferguson has often deployed Brian McClair in deeper positions, leaving Hughes as a solitary striker—a responsibility he positively thrives on.

The spectacular volley that helped Wales to shatter Spain 3–0 in a World Cup qualifying match in Wrexham in 1985 is perhaps Hughes' most memorable goal to date, but he played it down with typical modesty: 'With that sort of thing, either it goes in or you make a fool of yourself. Thankfully, it went in.'

Inevitably, Hughes has drawn comparisons with former Old Trafford greats, but he is possibly Manchester's finest home-grown talent since George Best. Now the United fans will want him to prove it.

REPORT by DES KELLY

From Portugal's conveyer belt . . .

A new rival for Real

AT one time, it was fashionable for Europe's big clubs to have at least one Portuguese player in their line-up. The French started the trend in the late 1960s, following Portugal's success in the 1966 World Cup Finals in England where they finished in third place.

As time progressed and the fortunes of Portugal's national side declined, so the talent drain dwindled. But the best of the Portuguese players still found

PAULO Futre of Portugal is all concentration here. He was the boy wonder of his country as he made his record-breaking debut at the age of seventeen-and-a-half.

their way to foreign pastures. For whatever the reputation of Portugal's footballers on the international transfer market, one feature has remained constant throughout their export lists—that of goalscorers.

From Alves to Gomes and, in more recent times, Chalana, Portugal has continued to produce a conveyer belt of outstanding striking talent. Paulo Futre is the latest in that line of succession.

Tall and elegant with lightning speed and exceptional dribbling skills, Futre has been described as his country's finest young prospect since the emergence of Fernando Chalana, Portugal's outstanding creative forward of the 1984 European Championships whose career since has been blighted by injury.

Futre, in his early twenties, has already picked up a wealth of experience at both club and international level. As a boy prodigy in September, 1985, he became the youngest player to represent his country—at the age of seventeen years, six months and twenty-one days—when he played in the 5–0 demolition of Finland.

He further enhanced his fledgling reputation in May, 1987, with a leading role in FC Porto's European Cup Final triumph over Bayern Munich.

Now, Futre is playing for Atletico Madrid following a £2.5 million transfer from FC Porto in July, 1987. Atletico see him as the man to lead them from the shadows of their more illustrious rivals, Real Madrid. Their confidence in him is based on an already impressive career of outstanding achievements and in the belief that the best is yet to come.

Futre, who was born on February 28, 1966, began his schoolboy football career with Sporting Lisbon at the age of twelve and made his first-team debut on a tour of Brazil in May, 1983.

He moved to FC Porto in the summer of 1984 and was an instant success, helping the club to break the long-standing domination of Benfica and Sporting Lisbon to win the Portuguese title in 1985 and again in 1986.

Following those twin triumphs came the first big disappointment of Futre's career during the 1986 Mexico World Cup Finals. He was upset not only by Portugal's embarrassing and dispute-ridden exit from the competition, but also by the surprising decision of coach Jose Torres to omit him from the national side's first-choice line-up.

Despite his peripheral role, Futre played impressively as a second-half substitute against England (won 1–0) and Poland (lost 1–0) to earn a starting place for the third game against Morocco. By that time, however, the players' internal wrangling with the Portuguese Federation over cash awards for their participation in the World Cup had taken its toll. Team morale was at rock bottom, and so were Portugal after an ignominious 3–1 defeat which sent them home in disgrace.

Futre and many of his team-mates involved in that Mexican humiliation restored some national pride a year later when they inspired FC Porto to European Cup triumph for the first time in their history. On a balmy spring evening in Vienna's Prater Stadium, Futre ascended new heights of power. He led the West German defence—and most notably his marker Pflugler—a merry dance

with his pace and power as FC Porto came from behind to win 2–1.

Futre's performance in Vienna made him one of the hottest properties in world football, and he was duly voted into the runners-up place behind Dutchman Ruud Gullit in the 1987 European Footballer of the Year awards. He could have had his pick of any number of big Continental clubs; instead he chose unfashionable Atletico Madrid, who offered him a contract even the likes of Barcelona and Juventus could not match.

Atletico, who had tried to sign him unsuccessfully two years earlier, had finally got their man. Yet Futre's first two seasons with Atletico were, like that of his side, a combination of the brilliant and inconsistent.

However, the award of the captain's armband in season 1988–89 showed recognition of his leadership qualities as well as his skills. Despite his slow start with Atletico, the club was still confident Futre would produce the goods.

Few men are better equipped than Paulo Futre to cope with the challenge of Spanish football and its array of steel-tight defences.

FUTRE was the star turn in the World XI against the Football League side to celebrate the League Centenary. Here is Paulo sliding past the off-balance Kenny Sansom.

GUNNERS AT THE DOUBLE

AFTER the most dramatic ending to the Championship in the history of the Football League, Arsenal were sitting on top of the world and looking forward to the Nineties. But can they emulate their glorious predecessors of the Seventies, whose peak achievement was an FA Cup-League "double"? MARK DEMUTH of the Sunday Express examines their prospects and also the views of Bob Wilson, goalkeeper in the famous 1971 team.

Will Arsenal be the Team of the Nineties?

'THERE is no point being one-season wonders. We must prove that this is the start of a golden era for the club.'

That was the blunt reaction of evergreen Irishman David O'Leary to the League title Arsenal clinched on a night of unforgettable drama at Liverpool on May 26, 1989.

For the record, Arsenal's stunning 2–0 win at a packed Anfield earned the Gunners their ninth championship. It also denied Liverpool a record eighteenth title and the completion of an equally astonishing second League and Cup 'double' in three years.

Liverpool's was an impressive achievement by any standard. But the sheer impact of that night of unbridled celebration and joy threatens to make a far

ABOVE George Graham receives the new Barclays Bank Manager of the Year trophy from Mr Bill Gordon, the bank's UK corporate director. The prize also included a Barclaycard Portfolio valued at £5,000.

OPPOSITE Time for celebration in the Arsenal dressing-room for Alan Smith, scorer of the first goal in the vital 2–0 win at Anfield.

greater impression than mere statistics on a page. It could be the result that dictates the course of English football into the next decade. What odds Arsenal . . . 'Team of The Nineties'?

England midfielder Michael Thomas, scorer of the injury-time goal that settled the tightest First Division title race in history, is just one of the talented group of home-grown youngsters at manager George Graham's disposal. Others with whom Arsenal's destiny lies are Thomas's fellow England internationals David Rocastle and Tony Adams, Paul Merson, the 1989 Young Player of the Year, and Lee Dixon, an 'outsider' who cost £400,000 from Stoke City.

Together they helped obliterate the stigma that had remained with Arsenal since their previous title success in 1971, the year Bertie Mee's revered side achieved the 'double'. It was next to that feat that subsequent Highbury successes would be measured.

Before May, 1989, there had been only two: the 1979 FA Cup and the 1987 Littlewoods Cup, won in Graham's first season. But neither honour matched Highbury demands.

The joyous scenes witnessed at Anfield when Arsenal finally crossed that tightrope of expectation were therefore understandable. Not only had Graham's team bridged a wide gulf, but they now had convincing proof that they were ready to end Liverpool's reign of supremacy.

Had the ghost of 1971 been exorcised? And would the glory of 1989 either inspire or intimidate Graham's troops? These were the questions that Arsenal faced when they began the defence of their title in the 1989–90 season.

George Graham, for one, was confident of steering his side to further success. 'We are still a young side and it will be another two years before we see the best from players like David Rocastle, Tony Adams and Michael Thomas,' says the Arsenal manager. 'That's a happy thought.'

Few disagreed with him. Not even stalwart David O'Leary, now in his thirties and whose career at Highbury is not expected to make much of an impression on the 1990s.

'I have a feeling Arsenal are going to stay at the top for a long time,' said the Republic of Ireland defender after collecting his first championship medal. 'David Rocastle was a revelation on the right wing, Michael Thomas came through superbly, while I thought Nigel Winterburn should have been rewarded by England for the form he showed.

'There are so many players who can safeguard the club's future,' said the man who had been a pillar of Arsenal's defence for so many years. O'Leary, though, reserved special praise for his central defensive partner and his successor as skipper, Tony Adams.

Apart from losing his England place to Nottingham Forest's immaculate defender Des Walker during that season of triumph, Adams had also contended

Graham has a group of

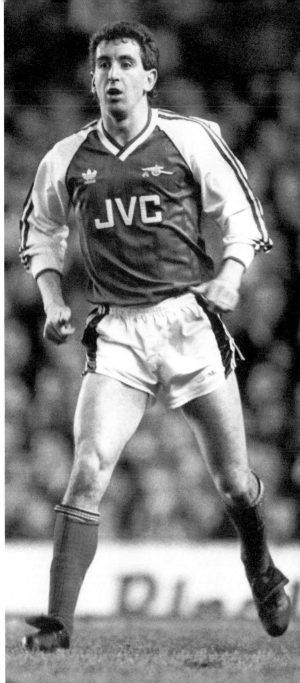

LEFT David O'Leary, the evergreen Irishman at Highbury, who was delighted to collect his first championship medal. ABOVE Nigel Winterburn, who showed England form during Arsenal's triumphant season in the opinion of O'Leary.

home-grown youngsters

with abuse from the terraces wherever he played. 'He deserves so much credit for what he went through,' said O'Leary of his team-mate, whose appearance at any ground was sure to provoke a cacophony of noise and derision from donkey impressionists in the crowd.

'He was only twenty-two but he ran a gauntlet of problems. Undoubtedly he emerged a stronger person and a better player.'

In recognising the 'young' threat to Liverpool's dominance, O'Leary was also quick to salute manager Graham. 'The main reason I am so confident about the future is because of him,' said O'Leary. 'He's a winner and the best. The perfect combination for a club like Arsenal.'

O'Leary's was not idle praise. The pair had had their differences at the start of season 1988–89. In fact O'Leary came close to jeopardising his chances of winning that elusive championship medal, and so completing his set of domestic honours, when he considered quitting the club after Graham had left him out of the side.

But O'Leary bore no grudge when he said: 'George should go down in history as one of the club's greatest managers. As far as the players are concerned, he went into Arsenal's hall of fame the night we beat Liverpool for the championship. I have been at Arsenal for sixteen years and he is the best manager I have played for.'

Bob Wilson, now a successful television presenter with the BBC, played beside Graham in Arsenal's famous 1971 'double-winning' side and is also a big fan of the Arsenal manager.

'In many ways, George Graham's team remind me of the side we played in and Bertie Mee managed,' says Wilson, the former Scottish international goalkeeper. 'The players believe in each other in the way we did.'

Such was Wilson's faith in his former team-mate's ability to return the League Championship to Highbury that he went on record as saying Arsenal would win the title six months before the drama of Anfield unfolded.

In a newspaper article dated November 30, 1988, Wilson said, after a morale-sapping Littlewoods Cup defeat to Liverpool: 'The Cups aren't that important to Arsenal this year. That defeat to Liverpool could be the making of their season and it is about time the title came back to London.' How right he proved!

Wilson's comparison between the class of 1971 and 1989 therefore makes interesting reading.

Talking about the midfield, Wilson says: 'There is definitely more variety and flair in the current team.' He points to the artistry and composure of players like Paul Davis and Michael Thomas as proof that Arsenal have shaken off the 'boring' tag which had hung like a noose prior to George Graham's arrival from Millwall as manager in 1986.

Wilson adds that Brian Marwood plays an uncannily similar role to the one

'The players believe in each other

George Armstrong had in the double-winning side. 'Both wide players would motor and cross the ball on a sixpence,' he says.

'The forwards are similar, too. Ray Kennedy was a great target man with a magic left foot, while John Radford was also strong, but Paul Merson is more mobile as is Alan Smith (*scorer of twenty-two invaluable League goals*). Merson, though weaker in the air, is like Radford in his ability to find space and hold the ball up.'

Of skipper Adams, Wilson says: 'Tony is getting better all the time. He is a natural talker and an enthusiastic captain.'

If Adams inspires Arsenal to greatness in the 1990s, no doubt few would begrudge him having the 'last bray'.

IT was all happening for young Michael Thomas in the months of April and May, 1989. On the LEFT, he is in action for England Under-21 against Albania. One month later, he is seeing if the League Trophy cap fits (RIGHT) after scoring the sensational injury-time goal at Anfield.

TWO more young Gunners with a bright outlook for Arsenal and England are David Roscastle (left) and Tony Adams, who is 'getting better all the time' according to Bob Wilson.

FOOTBALL HISTORY FOR DAVID PIZANTI AND ISRAEL

ISRAEL has been a nation with a greater-than-average propensity for making international news and writing history, dating back to its twelve Old Testament tribes, but as a power in the realms of football . . . hardly!

The name of Avi Cohen, a defender who played eighteen games for Liverpool in the early eighties, springs immediately to mind. But few have made as significant an impression as David Pizanti, a full-back whose domestic and international footballing ambitions have taken him on a soccer odyssey several times around the planet.

Pizanti, like most top Israeli players, began his career with the Tel Aviv club, where he quickly made an excellent impression. Soon his talent outgrew the relatively poor standard of Israeli club football and, with itchy feet, he started to look around for openings among the sport's more advanced countries.

At the time, he had a fierce desire to play in what he considers to be the two great footballing nations of the world, West Germany and England, and that desire led to the first leg of his round-the-world trek, when he secured a contract with Cologne in the West German First Division.

However, he failed to make the breakthrough into the Cologne first team and, in September, 1987, he took the brave step into the sophistication of West London, joining Queens Park Rangers for £150,000 having impressed their then manager Jim Smith.

Immediately, Pizanti declared himself to feeling at home in what he described as 'a fine, friendly, family club' and, although first-team appearances were few and far between, it seemed that his globe-trotting days may be coming to an end.

Indeed, during his short spell with QPR, he was able to sit back and wallow in the distinction that follows a player who has been involved in football in both England and West Germany. He made astute judgments about the differences between the two countries' game, saying: 'In England, matches are faster and tougher than in Germany, where the level of skill is higher. The English crowd gets good value because so much can happen in such a short space of time.'

He impressed many with his dogged determination to make progress in the rough-and-tumble world of English football. Of his struggle to hold down a place in the QPR side, he said: 'I just wanted to fight to stay in. All the time to play in the first team. I just had to try harder.'

But, as it transpired, Pizanti's travels were only just beginning. It quickly became clear that he was to be an integral part of his country's attempts to qualify for the 1990 World Cup Finals in Italy. Israel were in the Oceania Group—along with Australia and New Zealand—the winners of which qualified for a two-leg final against the winners of South American Group Two (Ecuador, Paraguay and Colombia).

The first assignment that was to launch Pizanti on his worldwide travels was a warm-up friendly against Wales in Tel Aviv which ended in a 3–3 draw.

However, the really crucial matches for World Cup qualification from the Oceania Group began against New Zealand and, thanks to a goal by Standard Liege striker Roni Rosenthal, they began with a 1–0 success. That was the game which Pizanti considers to be the highlight of his international career; he laid on the winning goal and played a solid role in the back four.

Australia were the next visitors to Israel and, due to a disputed late penalty from Eli Ohana of the Belgian side Mechelen, the spoils were shared.

Auckland was Pizanti's next port of call, and a 2–2 draw with New Zealand meant that, going into the final match in Sydney, Israel required just one point from the Australians (who needed a win) to secure the coveted play-off spot and the chance of a plum tie against a glamorous South American side.

That draw was achieved, for although the Australians scored in the late stages of the game, Ohana had already given Israel an all-important, first-half lead.

So Israel's quest for World Cup glory continued and Pizanti's opportunities for world travel were widened, with the impossible dream of victory over England in the grand final! It would compensate for all those endless airborne hours and days for Pizanti, whose footballing ambitions have overcome his rooted dislike of flying.

REPORT by PETER DRURY

Dean of Derby is up with the stars

DEAN SAUNDERS' most embarrassing moment came when an impromptu impression of former Swansea manager John Toshack went horribly wrong. The Welsh legend was standing in earshot at the time . . .

Fortunately for the lively Derby County striker, his impersonation of Toshack in the Welsh attack has gone down much better. So much so that Ian Rush and Mark Hughes, the swashbuckling successors to the recently-appointed Real Madrid coach, are glancing nervously over their shoulders at the man stealing up on the international hard shoulder.

Season 1988–89 proved the catalyst in Saunders' career. He made his international debut against the Republic of Ireland in March, 1986, but did not establish himself until three seasons later, when he was ever-present for Wales and increased his haul of caps to fourteen.

Up to the end of that season, Saunders had always been deployed wide on the right whenever he joined forces with Rush and Hughes. But such was his rapid development that neither of these two formidable rivals could be complacent about keeping his central attacking role.

A £1 million transfer from Oxford United to Derby in October, 1988, had confirmed Saunders' growing reputation before he went on to score fourteen League goals in Derby's best season for thirteen years—they finished 1988–89 fifth in the First Division—and further boosted his status.

On reflection, it is hard to believe that his career at Derby began in acrimony, after his seven-figure transfer had stirred a pot brimming with animosity and

DETERMINATION personified is Dean Saunders of Derby County and Wales.

resentment. Few had seen further than the father-son relationship that existed between the deal's chief protagonists, Derby chairman Robert Maxwell and his Oxford counterpart and son Kevin Maxwell.

While controversy raged off the field, Saunders had to take a back seat. But when let loose to express himself on the field, he grabbed all the 'right' headlines. Six goals in his first five games helped douse the flames his move had started. And it is indicative of the former Swansea City and Brighton and Hove Albion player's composure, both in front of goal and away from the action, that when the smoke cleared he had emerged as a goalscorer of the highest repute.

In stature the 'boy from Swansea' would remain behind Rush and Hughes; he was still the third man of the Welsh attack. But his goalscoring prowess in 1988–89 left his more illustrious rivals in the shade.

Rush scored only six League goals, and although Hughes did match Saunders' League total, he, unlike the Derby player, had started the season in the First Division. Saunders had found the Second Division target four times before Robert Maxwell even thought about opening his cheque book.

In Saunders' eyes he had arrived. 'Before that season I had suffered something of an inferiority complex,' he says. 'Rush and Hughes are two of the best strikers in the world, and of course I looked up to them. But after joining Derby, I did not seem to be so much in awe of them.

'At last I seemed to be emerging from their shadows. It made a change to hear people talking about competition for places in the Welsh attack and I could begin to feel on level terms.'

Should he continue in such breathtaking style, it should not be long before he too enjoys the back-handed compliment he gave Toshack by mimicking him. Like Toshack, Saunders has the potential to be remembered as a Welsh 'great'.

ABOVE Supersub Ian Rush on target for Liverpool in the extra-time Cup Final thriller against Everton.

Michel magic

By JOHN PRICE

'I have a special and natural talent for football'

IN an age when work-rate, physical prowess, bottomless lungs and hydraulic legs appear to be the qualities most admired in and required from footballers, it is fitting that one of the world's most valuable players should insist that nothing can match natural gifts and skills.

Jose Miguel Gonzalez Maria del Campo, better known simply as Michel, believes he has been blessed with natural talents. He says so, yet he manages to draw a distinct line between honesty and boasting. But then, the gifted Real Madrid midfielder does not need to blow his own trumpet.

Boyish good looks and a tall athletic figure, allied to a swashbuckling style of play, have brought him the title of 'El niño dorado', the Golden Boy of Spanish football, as well as favourable comparisons with the legendary French outside-right Raymond Kopa, who dominated the Bernabeu flanks for Real during the late 1950s.

Michel has all the hallmarks of quality that were stamped throughout the great side in which Kopa starred, combining speed, skill and the ability to beat defenders on Real's right wing.

Indeed, such was Michel's burgeoning reputation following the 1988 European Championships, in which he emerged as one of the outstanding individuals of the tournament despite Spain's poor showing, that Real effectively secured his playing services for life—and also ended speculation of a possible move to Italy—with a lucrative seven-year contract.

The deal duly catapulted Michel into the millionaire superstar bracket, a far cry from the poverty of the working-class suburbs of Los Angeles where he grew up. Yet despite those humble beginnings the young Michel, who played his early football amid the rubble of derelict houses, never doubted he would reach the top of the football ladder.

'My problem has never been a lack of confidence,' he says. 'Without sounding boastful, I have to admit that I have a special and natural talent for football.'

Those special talents were spotted by his childhood idols Real Madrid, whose youth sections he joined at the age of fifteen. He made steady progress through the ranks, despite incurring the wrath of many of the coaches with his precocity and super-confident approach.

'At the start of my career with Real,' he says, 'I was branded as something of a rebel because I always thought I knew better than the coaches. I guess I was just too full of myself in those days but eventually they managed to

MICHEL is the Golden Boy of Spanish football— and Real Madrid rate him highly enough for a seven-year contract.

TOGETHER IN THE NURSERY

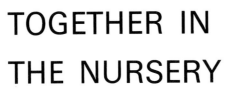

THREE superstars who served in the same Castilla "nursery" as Michel. They are Martin Vasquez (left), Emilio Butragueno (below) and Chendo (opposite). All four were capped almost simultaneously.

make me settle down and play more as a member of the team than as an individual.'

In 1981 Michel, then eighteen, joined Real's nursery side Castilla and quickly established himself on the right wing. A year later he was joined by Emilio Butragueno, Chendo, Manuel Sanchis and Martin Vazquez and they all progressed into the Real first team and the national side at around the same time. Of this group, only Martin Vazquez was not in the Spanish Under-21 side which lost to England in the European Championship Final of 1984.

Michel won a regular place on the right side of the Real midfield in season 1984–85, despite a three-match suspension and a £500 club fine for being sent off in a league game against Hercules.

However, he fully justified the faith shown in him by coach Luis Molowny with a devastating performance against Videoton in the first leg of the UEFA Cup Final, scoring the first goal and creating further goals for Santillana and Valdano in a 3–0 victory in Hungary.

Michel started the following season in similarly expansive form and made his international debut in a goalless draw with Austria in November 1985. Although he was unable to make any impact on that occasion, he made amends a month later with his first international goal for Spain, a spectacular free-kick, in a 2–0 victory over Bulgaria.

Real's dramatic upturn in fortunes in 1985–86, when they regained the League title after an absence of six years and retained the UEFA Cup, owed much to Michel's skilful runs and crosses from the right.

At the end of that season came the Mexico World Cup, in which Michel achieved international fame, not to say notoriety, when his spectacular volley in Spain's opening group game against Brazil was not allowed, despite the later video evidence that the ball had crossed the goal-line.

Spain, with Michel in outstanding form, recovered from that early setback to reach the quarter-finals before suffering a shock defeat on penalties by an unfancied Belgium side.

Michel's performances in Mexico brought a fanfare of accolades from all over the globe but he was less than satisfied. He said: 'Although I did not play too badly, I should have created more chances, particularly against Belgium. We should have beaten them easily.'

The second major disappointment of Michel's career came in April, 1989, when Real crashed out of the European Cup in the semi-finals to the eventual champions AC Milan on a 6–1 aggregate. The feeling of failure was acute, so

that the winning of a third successive league title only slightly compensated. Such is the tradition of European success at the Bernabeu that Real's fans still demand more than just domestic success.

The burden of the past is a heavy one, but '*El niño dorado*' has one advantage. In a country where most of the great midfielders—from Puskas to Kopa, through Neeskens and Breitner to Cruyff and Schuster—were all foreigners, he is a local hero. And being in his mid-twenties, he has time on his side. With the arrival of John Toshack as manager in July, 1989, heralding a new dynasty at the Bernabeu, Michel may well yet emulate Kopa and that legendary Real side.

MECHELEN RIDING HIGH

A FEW years ago the mention of Mechelen, a small city in the Flemish-speaking region of Belgium, would scarcely have encouraged thoughts of a thriving European football power.

Since winning the Belgian Championship three times in six years during the mid-1940s, Mechelen had fallen into the bracket of perennial strugglers, watched by crowds of fewer than 8,000. The highlight of their achievement was either to avoid relegation to the second division or, when they had gone down, to claw their way back.

That was until May, 1988, when KV Mechelen stamped their mark on the map of European football with a shock 1–0 victory over the defending champions and pre-match favourites Ajax to win the Cup-Winners Cup in Strasbourg.

The decisive second-half goal from the tall Dutch forward Piet Den Boer—the only surviving member of the club's second division days—enabled Mechelen to carry off the trophy in what was, remarkably, their first-ever taste of European competition.

Mechelen furthered their reputation in February, 1989, by beating the then Champions' Cup holders PSV Eindhoven, to carry off the European Super Cup. During the same season, they also established superiority on the domestic front, breaking the 'old guard' domination of Anderlecht and Club Brugge to clinch the League title for the first time since 1948 and thus secure an inaugural appearance in the Champions' Cup for 1989–90.

But what should have been a joyous occasion for everyone connected with the club was overshadowed by the departure of their influential Dutch coach, Aad De Mos, who took over control of their bitter rivals, the fallen giants of Anderlecht.

Mechelen's feeling of loss was acute. For it was the arrival of De Mos in 1985 which brought a dramatic upturn in the club's playing fortunes. De Mos had, in fact, just taken Ajax to the Dutch League title when he found his services were no longer required; a series of internal wrangles with several of the players forced his departure.

BUT THEY'LL MISS
MAESTRO DE MOS

AGAIN . . .

STIRRING times for the born-again Mechelen, seen here having a ball Belgian-style after the Cup-Winners' Cup victory over Ajax in 1988.

Within twelve months of joining Mechelen, De Mos had turned them into one of the three leading Belgian club sides. The transformation was remarkable. They beat FC Liege in the Belgian Cup Final of 1987—courtesy of a Den Boer goal—to secure their first silverware under De Mos's command and win a place in Europe.

De Mos's policy of introducing talented young players to the side, as well as shrewd buying on the transfer market, had reaped handsome dividends, and none was more successful than striker Eli Ohana, signed from Beiter Jerusalem for £250,000. The Israeli international quickly repaid his transfer fee with fifteen goals in his first season; he followed it a year later, in 1987–88, with some crucial strikes in the Cup-Winners Cup as well as creating Den Boer's winner against Ajax in the Final.

Mechelen's greatest strength, however, was their defence, which produced three new international stars for Belgium in goalkeeper Michel Preud'homme, the 1987 Belgian Footballer of the Year, stopper Leo Clijsters and Geert Deferm.

The style of play De Mos had created at Mechelen, combining a steel-tight defence with a heavy reliance on counter-attack, was perfectly suited to the

cut-and-thrust technique of European competition. This was illustrated by the fact that Mechelen were unbeaten throughout their run to the final, which included three victories on foreign soil.

With the profits from Mechelen's cup glory, De Mos again invested shrewdly, spending £800,000 on Dutch forward John Bosman, a member of Holland's triumphant European Championship squad. Bosman topped the club's scoring charts with eighteen goals as Mechelen carried off their first Belgium League title for forty-one years.

The goals of Bosman also helped Mechelen to claim the European Super Cup, the talented striker scoring twice to complete a 3–1 aggregate victory.

But the 1989–89 season was not without its disappointments for Mechelen, who lost their grip on the Cup-Winners Cup, the competition which had brought them international fame. Having established a 2–1 home advantage in the semi-finals against the Italian Cup holders Sampdoria, they held on for more than seventy minutes in the return leg, only to concede three goals in the last eighteen minutes.

However, the feeling of disappointment at losing their European crown bore no comparison to that over De Mos's departure. The fact that the club failed to hold on to their brilliant coach suggested that, while Mechelen were no longer 'also rans' in Belgium, Anderlecht, despite their recent slump, still remained the nation's leading club.

Mechelen turned to another Dutchman as De Mos's successor in May, 1989 — the legendary Holland defender Rudi Krol. His task was indeed a daunting one; to consolidate and improve upon the success of De Mos and ultimately, to claim the biggest honour of all, the European Cup.

Only time would tell if it would prove to be an impossible legacy.

ABOVE Happy winner Den Boer of Mechelen, scorer of vital goals in the triumphs of the past two years.

Bobby is back where he belongs

By DENNIS SIGNY, OBE (The Times)

CONSIDERING that he has been around the soccer circuit for a lifetime, it has taken Bobby Campbell a long time to be 'discovered'.

When Chelsea's chairman Ken Bates called on Campbell to try and restore order at a troubled Stamford Bridge, he was not regarded as a 'big name' in managerial terms by many in football. Yet the fifty-year-old saviour of Chelsea has an excellent *curriculum vitae*. He blooded international players such as Liam Brady, David O'Leary, Frank Stapleton and Graham Rix into the Arsenal league side as youngsters when he was the coach at Highbury. He also handled superstars of the calibre of George Best, Bobby Moore and Rodney Marsh when he was the manager of Fulham.

Campbell is a bubbly, extrovert Liverpudlian who has experienced the ups and downs of the football world . . . and has always bounced back to the top. But, in football terms, he was never a superstar manager.

When the headline writers glorified El Tel or The Doc or Supermac or Cloughie, everyone knew to whom they referred. The best Bobby ever managed was the inevitable 'Campbell's Kingdom' headline when things were going well . . . or 'Campbell's in the soup' when they weren't.

He was one of twelve children brought up in the tough Scotland Road area

of Liverpool. His neighbours and boyhood pals were Jimmy Melia, also to become a footballer and a colourful FA Cup Final manager with Brighton, and comedian Jimmy Tarbuck.

Liverpool signed Bobby as a schoolboy, and he became a ground-staff lad and then a professional in his eight years at Anfield from 1954. His leadership qualities stood out and he was chosen to captain the England youth side at under-sixteen and under-eighteen level.

Bobby Charlton was with him in the under-sixteens. Duncan Edwards, the Manchester United and England protegé who died in the Munich air disaster, played alongside him at youth level.

Campbell moved on to Portsmouth but, at the age of twenty-eight his playing career was cut short by serious ligament injury and he started on the coaching side of the game at Fratton Park.

Gordon Jago, then managing Queens Park Rangers, noted his potential in 1970 and he switched to the West London club as a coach and helped transform it into one of the brightest footballing sides in the Football League.

Terry Venables was a player with Rangers at the time and he acknowledged Campbell's coaching methods. Later, Venables declared that he learned a lot that was to be useful to him in his career at Crystal Palace, QPR, Barcelona and Tottenham Hotspur.

Bobby moved to Highbury in 1973 as deputy to Bertie Mee, the manager who had guided Arsenal to the League and Cup double, and further enhanced his reputation as a top coach.

When Mee left and he did not get the manager's job, Campbell switched to Fulham. In his first experience as a manager, he showed the wheeler-dealer qualities that benifited Chelsea so well in his first year.

GOLDEN oldies of Bobby Campbell's days at Fulham, where he handled two Craven Cottage favourites in Rodney Marsh and (below) Bobby Moore.

He was four years at Craven Cottage—and carried on the good work when he moved to Portsmouth. Not only did he sign for bargain fees Mark Hateley and Neil Webb, two of England manager Bobby Robson's World Cup squad, he also led Pompey out of the doldrums of the Third Division.

Months later he was sacked . . . and entered an unhappy period of his life. Although he coached in Kuwait for two years and had a few months helping Frank Sibley when he was managing at QPR, he had to wait three years before a court action against Portsmouth achieved a financial settlement.

He was in his third spell at QPR, as reserve team coach, when he got the call to Chelsea. And, although he refused to get carried away by the record-breaking season that brought the Second Division championship to Stamford Bridge, he utilised all his experience and know-how to help bring back the glory days.

He became Chelsea's manager at the start of the First Division play-off games at the end of the 1987–88 season, and although he was unable to prevent the side going down, the improvement showed almost immediately on his arrival. At the end of his first year in charge, he was voted the Second Division Manager of the Year with this impressive League record: Played 54, Won 30, Drew 17, Lost 7, Goals For 104, Goals Against 61.

After an unimpressive start to the 1988–89 season, with only three points gathered from the first six games. Chelsea started to take off. A 2–0 win at Leeds, with John Bumstead scoring an important goal off the back of his heel, put the show on the road. Campbell reckoned that the 3–0 win at Stoke with ten men, after Peter Nicholas had been sent off in the opening minutes of the game, was their performance of the season. He was delighted that the long-serving Bumstead's goal against Leeds at home clinched the title.

Campbell's side went a record twenty-seven games without defeat and won the championship in a canter from Manchester City with a record ninety-nine points. 'He's here for life if he wants to be,' said chairman Bates.

Campbell, perhaps remembering his Portsmouth experience, refused to be carried away. He agreed a new and improved contract, but pointed out that Chelsea were only back where they were when he had taken over—in the top division. But he established a good rapport with the Chelsea supporters and sang their praises as they travelled all over the country and roared their team home.

'Relegation was a shock to the system for everyone,' he said. 'It had been on the cards and you have to take stock of yourself. What needed changing was attitude of minds. Whether players are winning or losing, they go to bed each night with the same skill. Good players don't become bad players overnight.

'My main job was to get the maximum output from those players every

CONGRATULATIONS to Campbell on becoming Barclays League Divisional Manager of the Season. Here he is, left to right, with Division Four winner Billy McEwan (Rotherham), John Quinton (chairman of Barclays), and Third Division winner Graham Turner (Wolves).

time they played. If you have good players, plus a good attitude, you have a chance.'

He bought well. Graham Roberts, an inspirational captain who became Chelsea's Player of the Year, and Peter Nicholas were imported from Scotland for less than Everton paid Chelsea for Pat Nevin.

Even though Campbell paid out a club record £725,000 for goalkeeper Dave Beasant, and signed Dave Mitchell and Kenneth Monkou from Feyenoord as squad players, he still balanced the books. Once a wheeler-dealer . . .

Grandfather Bobby—his eldest son Greg, a striker with Plymouth Argyle, had a child during the season—talks basic commonsense about his role. 'You have to be a shop-floor psychiatrist,' he says. 'If you have four players unhappy that they are not in the team, that is their fault. If there are sixteen, it's yours.'

Campbell considers that there are three 'leagues' in the First Division. Liverpool are on their own, then there are a few teams expected to win something, then there are the others hoping to stay in the division. He hopes Chelsea are big enough to be in the second category.

Manchester City and **Crystal Palace**, after their play-off success, accompanied Chelsea into the top flight in 1989. Both are managed by bright young coaches, City's Mel Machin and Steve Coppell at Palace.

ABOVE Vital new signings for Chelsea were Kenneth Monkou from Feyenoord (left) and Dave Beasant (right) from Wimbledon via Newcastle at high speed.

City's young side showed their nerves at a crucial stage in the promotion race; Palace, with Ian Wright and Mark Bright contributing fifty-eight goals, made it after a nail-biting finish. Bobby Campbell was pleased because Palace finished third on merit. He abhors the play-off system he had to endure when he took over at Chelsea the previous year.

PLAYER OF THE YEAR

INSPIRING captain and super signing was Graham Roberts, deservedly voted player of the Year by Chelsea fans.

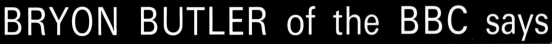

BRYON BUTLER of the BBC says

Chelsea, once in your system, are an unbreakable addiction . . .

ALL that Chelsea have needed to regain their place in the First Division and keep their home at Stamford Bridge is talent, experience, courage, expertise, high and low cunning, invention, profound conviction, passion, audacity, gladiatorial aggression, a touch of jungle warfare, early mornings and late nights, expensive counsel, boundless generosity, resilience, stamina and undentable optimism.

It also took team-work involving everyone from the Patriarch to Lady Thresa and her kettle beyond price in that noisy asylum the club are pleased to call offices.

The exciting Campbell clan needed less than the full season to win their promotion but it required a tough replay or two to keep out Marler Rovers. There was the odd hiccup away from home—including Scunthorpe of blessed memory—but it is not in the nature of Chelsea to do things without a whisper of drama.

The events of promotion year have simply emphasised why Chelsea are a club worth sweating a few magnums of blood for. Clubs have characters as different and readily identifiable as thumbprints and accents; and Chelsea take their place in footballing society as a club with stylish differences, a club which relishes a gamble, a club which is prepared to live a little dangerously and a club which has elevated unpredictability into an art form. Chelsea, once in your system, are an unbreakable addiction.

What else would you expect from a club that was created as speedily as a cup of instant coffee? At the start of 1905 the club did not exist. Its first meeting was on 14 March; their first players were signed on 26 April 'subject to Chelsea being elected to the League'; and on 29 May the League's annual meeting was persuaded 'you really cannot refuse us.' Bingo! Standing start to League status in five months without playing a single game. Chelsea, obviously, were going to be no ordinary club.

'Blue is the Colour'

The history of the club is even sandwiched between two cloud-capped goalkeepers. They take their place at either end of Chelsea's long and soul-stirring parade of players like giant book-ends.

In the beginning, one of their first signings was Billy 'Fatty' Foulke, 6ft 2in and 22 stone, the club's first captain and a huge, lovable rascal who once declared: 'I don't care what you call me so long as you don't call me late for lunch.'

And, of course, propping up the other end of the Chelsea story, a little taller than Foulke and a pound or two lighter, is Dave Beasant. Dave arrived at The Bridge by a devious route—Edgware Town, Wimbledon, Newcastle and a courtesy call on every League ground in the country—but Chelsea were always a good bet for him. He said he missed London's traffic jams, so where better than the Kings Road.

One or two things have happened since Dave replaced Billy. The League Championship, the FA Cup, the League Cup and the European Cup Winners Cup have all been won. The Shed has swayed, swooned and sometimes sworn ('Blue is the Colour') at the likes of Gallacher, Lawton, Walker and Goulden, through to Greavsie, Ossie, Chopper and Butch and to Mr Campbell's admirable Class of '89.

A football club like Chelsea, however, is more than a limited company with employees who kick and trap a ball on a pitch surrounded by dutch barns and a few outhouses. A club like Chelsea is an amalgam of its traditions and memories, ambitions and fears, successes and failures. It is the creation of all the people who have cared passionately about it down through the years—above all its supporters.

A club like Chelsea also knows that in moments of high stress the right man will emerge to pull it back on to its feet.

It is doubtful, even so, if the old club anticipated someone quite like Ken Bates galloping up on a white charger. But they must have recognised each other as kindred souls because the marriage was clearly arranged by a higher authority.

CONGRATULATIONS.

OPPOSITE Dave Beasant ('Chelsea were always a good bet for him'). BELOW Chairman Ken Bates ('galloping up on a white charger').

The marriage was clearly arranged by a higher authority . . .

THIS
LIFE,

IS YOUR JOHN TOSHACK!

Presenting the big red book is ALEX SPINK (Daily Telegraph)

'JOHN TOSHACK is intelligent and articulate. He is not one of those people who thinks he knows it all. It is evident to me that he has the potential to go to the top.'

So said *MALCOLM STRUHL*, the former chairman of Swansea City, on the day he appointed you as the youngest manager in the Football League at the age of twenty-nine. And, as your exploits since have shown, he wasn't a bad judge of character.

John Benjamin Toshack, born in Cardiff on March 22, 1949, and who grew up to be manager of Real Madrid—the world's most famous club side—this is your life.

From an early age at home with father George, a carpenter, and mother Joan, you showed you had a talent for the game, setting a Cardiff schoolboy record by scoring forty-seven goals in one season.

You then announced yourself on the international stage by notching a hat-trick in your first appearance in a Wales shirt, at schoolboy level. Four more schoolboy caps followed before you joined Cardiff City, the team you had supported as a boy.

Yet, it is said, even in those early days you had your goals plotted out—to play for Read Madrid and to manage Liverpool!

The impact you made at Cardiff was immediate. You scored within a minute of coming on as a substitute against Leyton Orient on your debut in November, 1965, when you were just sixteen years old.

Seventy-eight goals in 174 appearances for Cardiff attracted the interest of one *BOBBY ROBSON*, now England manager but, at the time, boss of Fulham. However, you rejected the West Londoners' overtures and instead chose Liverpool, who parted with £110,000 for your services.

The figure was an Anfield club record but you gave manager Bill Shankly no cause for regret during your spell on Merseyside. In all, you played 208 times for Liverpool and scored eighty-five goals.

In that time, you overcame a serious injury which threatened to cut short your playing career. An intended £100,000 transfer to Leicester City in November, 1974, fell through when the medical showed you to be suffering from calcification of the left thigh. That must have been a difficult time for you?

'Yes, it was. Whenever I jumped to head a ball, I used the left leg to propel myself into the air, and it was the tendons in this leg that were strained. For eighteen months before City came to sign me, I had been aware I had the injury, but it was a shock to find out from the medical examination that Leicester considered I was unfit.'

But following a successful operation, you blasted the doubters with thirty goals in fifty-two games. 'Yes, that was the consistency I was after and I was determined to keep it going until I was recognised as the best in my position in the country.'

You were certainly the best in Wales at the time. In a ten-year international career stretching to 1979, you played forty times at centre-forward and scored thirteen goals, including a magnificent hat-trick in a 3–0 win against Scotland.

Your reward for sterling services to Liverpool was a free transfer in 1978. You were quickly snapped up by Swansea as player-manager, so starting a remarkable association with the South Wales club. You took them from the Fourth Division to the First in just thirty-eight months—the first Welsh club to reach the top flight for twenty years—and on December 16, 1981, the club sat proudly on top of the pile. An MBE from Her Majesty The Queen saluted your efforts.

'Each summer after we won promotion, Tosh took a cold, clinical look at the side and then went out and bought new men to replace lads who had done well,' remembers *JEREMY CHARLES*, who played under Toshack at the Vetch Field. 'That, to my mind, was the mark of a great manager.'

You transferred *DAVE RUSHBURY* to Carlisle United during this time, but he still remembers you fondly. 'The Toshack secret lay in man-management. His ability to keep players happy and content even when they weren't in the side.

'John had an uncanny knack of knowing just when an individual is about to hit a rough patch—and acting accordingly. The result was that players responded to him. They accepted that what he was doing was always in the best interests of the side.'

But events took a nasty turn at the Vetch. Swansea were twice relegated

BOB Paisley, an old colleague of Toshack, says Toshack has the passion and fervour associated with the Welsh.

as mounting debts crippled the club and you, despite being labelled the 'Manager of the Century' by the late *BILL SHANKLY*, lost your job. However, you re-surfaced two months later, in the somewhat unlikely setting of Portugal, as coach of Sporting Lisbon.

'When I was at Liverpool, Bill Shankly said: "Even if you're going to sweep the road, sweep it well." Everything I do I want to do well and I was determined that I would bounce back after leaving Swansea.'

You most certainly did that. A successful season in Portugal preceded four outstanding years as manager of Real Sociedad in the Basque region of Spain. In your second season in San Sebastian, you steered Sociedad to the first Spanish Cup success in their seventy-five-year history.

And then came the call from Real Madrid. Bill Shankly, who had once said, 'John's success fills me with pride, but it doesn't surprise me. You see, he knows the recipe,' would have been so proud.

BOB PAISLEY, an old colleague of yours at Liverpool, says you have the passion and fervour that is always associated with the Welsh. But you also have that little bit extra, that edge that has made you the manager of the world's top football club.

John Toshack, this is your life.

ABOVE Jeremy Charles, who played under Toshack at Swansea, says that his secret was knowing when to replace lads who had done well.

'Does not fit easily into the image of superstar . . .'

Jim Leighton under the microscope

by JASON TOMAS

Sunday Times

EACH SUMMER, Alan Hodgkinson runs a coaching clinic for promising young Scottish goalkeepers at the Inverclyde national sports centre in the west coast resort of Largs. One of his teaching aids is a video recording of famous goals, including one conceded by the Manchester United 'keeper Jim Leighton when Scotland lost 1–0 to England at Wembley in May, 1988.

All that separated the two teams that afternoon was the brilliant ingenuity of Peter Beardsley as he took the ball, rapier-like, through the Scotland defence and left Leighton in the unenviable situation of being the only man left to beat. To most people, no 'keeper on earth could have stopped Beardsley's decisive strike. But Hodgkinson, re-playing the goal in slow motion, implores his audience to be ultra critical.

'I want you to ask yourself: What could I have done better if I had been in Jim's position?' he tells them. The plea provokes a murmur of surprise, but Hodgkinson persists. 'Don't you think Jim might have waited a little longer before committing himself?'

Leighton would be the last person to quibble about being put under the microscope in this way. He is used to it, because he himself has worked closely with Hodgkinson ever since the former Sheffield United and England 'keeper joined the Scottish Football Association's coaching staff in 1986. Hence the fact that Leighton, much to the astonishment of those who have become used to poking fun at Scottish 'keepers, has become one of the most respected in Europe.

At first glance, Leighton does not fit easily into the image of superstar goalkeeper, and not just because of the fallibility of the poor souls who have preceded him north of the border. He wears contact lenses, and another source of embarrassment to him are his bandy legs.

The contact lenses are a sore subject with him, especially since his experience of losing one, and thus needing to be substituted, during a crucial World Cup qualifying tie against Wales. As for those legs, he recalls that he underwent remedial exercise classes for years but eventually gave up when he noticed

Should Jim have waited a little longer ?

THIS is the action picture so often put to Jim Leighton by master coach Alan Hodgkinson. It is Peter Beardsley's winning goal against Scotland at Wembley in 1988.

that the Rangers winger, Willie Henderson, one of his favourite players, had the same deformity. In Leighton's case, it has given him such a laboured running style that his first Aberdeen manager, Ally Macleod, referred to him tongue in cheek as Brendan Foster.

'I am the world's worst runner,' Leighton says, 'but I like to think I am like Willie Miller (*the Aberdeen and Scotland central defender*). He is not a good runner either, but you try and beat him over the distance that matters.'

Among those who readily confirm Leighton's appearances-can-be-deceptive point are Alex Ferguson, once his Aberdeen and Scotland manager, and the Scotland coach, Andy Roxburgh. Ferguson had no compunction about buying Leighton for Manchester United for £850,000 in the summer of 1988, despite his lack of experience in England and the intense pressures on those who fill such important positions at such big clubs.

Roxburgh looks upon him as one of the few genuine world-class players available to the national team following the retirement of Graeme Souness and Kenny Dalglish from the international scene. Leighton, who is thirty-one, gained his fiftieth cap against Chile at the end of the 1988–89 season, and seems likely to emulate Dalglish by reaching the target of one hundred caps.

The other man, of course, who can vouch for Leighton's expertise is Alan Hodgkinson. Leighton had been a Scotland player for three years when he started working with Hodgkinson. It was an important turning point for the player because he felt he had reached a stage in his career where he badly needed someone to push him in order to develop further.

As the most senior of Aberdeen's goalkeepers, he had been responsible for supervising the day-to-day training of the others. 'I was happy to do this,' he recalls, 'but it did tend to detract from my own work.'

Leighton says that Hodgkinson forced him to become more self-demanding in terms of the finer points of his job, and not just because of the coach's knowledge and dour, hard-to-please Yorkshire personality. To Hodgkinson, an equally relevant factor is his practice of raising the number of goalkeepers in the Scotland squad for pre-match training sessions to four and sometimes six. 'It has created a more competitive atmosphere among the 'keepers,' he says.

Leighton's emergence as an outstanding 'keeper has been perfectly timed from Scotland's point of view—it has coincided with a period in which the rebuilding of their team has inevitably caused them to be more vulnerable.

But significantly, their goals-against record has been excellent. Only Belgium have scored more than two goals against Leighton. They first did it in 1982, when winning 3–2.

Rather more difficult for Leighton to accept was Belgium's 4–1 win in Brussels in April, 1987, Scotland's heaviest defeat since Brazil beat them by the same score in the 1982 World Cup.

Leighton agrees with Hodgkinson that at least one of the Belgium goals could be attributed to his being slow to react to their explosive breaks. But he finds it impossible to rationalise his performance. His ability to maintain concentration—one of the advantages of his mild-mannered, equable nature—has always been looked upon as one of his strong points.

When assessing the stature he has achieved, Leighton, who spends much of his spare time with the Scotland squad reading or battling with Richard Gough on his chess computer, feels that he had the ideal upbringing. He considers himself fortunate that although he was an only child, his parents took care not to spoil him; that after leaving school with six 0-levels, he gained a more realistic view of life than many other professional footballers by working in his local unemployment benefits office; and that Eric Sorensen, a former Danish international 'keeper, was manager of the junior team for which he played—Dalry Thistle—before joining Aberdeen in 1977.

'Any success I have had in the game would not have been possible without all the help and encouragement Eric gave me during the early part of my career,' Leighton says. 'I just hope he gets a lot of pride from what I have achieved.'

Home-bread skills of Jurgen Klinsmann

By MARK DEMUTH

JURGEN KLINSMANN is without doubt the rising star of West German football and his £1.3 million transfer to Italian champions Internazionale in the 1989 close season should further enhance his sparkling reputation.

However, not so well documented is Klinsmann's skill in the kitchen, where he has mastered the art of baking bread. It is a talent he acquired at an early age. His parents ran a bakery in his home town of Stuttgart and Jurgen, one of four sons, learned the trade.

Oddly enough, his parents' time-consuming occupation had a beneficial effect on Klinsmann. In the hours the Klinsmanns spent baking loaves, he became very independent and this was particularly apparent when he started to realise his potential in football's searing oven.

The young forward, having had to fend for himself from an early age, thrived on the responsibility and expectation heaped on him after VfB Stuttgart signed him in 1984 at the age of twenty.

Five years later, he was to put his resilience to the ultimate test by attempting to overcome the pressures and demands of Italian club football. The imposing shadow cast by Inter's grand San Siro stadium is sufficient to reduce lesser players to near breakdown stage, but Klinsmann was undeterred.

The opportunity to link up beside international team-mates Lothar Matthaus and Andreas Brehme proved only a bonus, not the overriding factor, in his decision to join Internazionale. Their presence would certainly help him settle, but Klinsmann is one to shy away from burdening people with his problems.

OPPOSITE Happiness is a man called Jurgen Klinsmann, after he had scored for Stuttgart in the UEFA Cup Final thriller against ultimate winners Napoli.

'I would rather make my own mistakes,' he once said, which is an indication of his single-minded approach.

This attitude of mind came to the fore during the 1988 European Championship Finals in West Germany. The penetrating runs he made deep into opponents' halves were a feature of West Germany's progress to the semi-finals.

The hosts were beaten at that stage by Holland, the eventual champions, but Klinsmann had still managed to leave his mark on the game. An enterprising run, in which he cleverly beat two men before falling under a challenge from Holland's Frank Rijkaard, had enabled Matthaus to put the Germans ahead from the penalty spot—but two late goals took the Dutch through to the final.

Even so, the blond, bustling striker had emerged as one of West Germany's outstanding successes in the Finals and a cluster of clubs soon became interested in the six-foot forward. Klinsmann's appearance in the Olympic Games three months later marked the end of an incredible year for the new German hope.

It had begun in December 1987, when he celebrated his international debut on a South American tour against Brazil. He finished that season as the German Bundesliga's top scorer with nineteen goals and was also voted Footballer of the Year.

Those goals were enough to earn Stuttgart a place in the 1988–89 UEFA Cup and they did not disappoint by reaching the final in which they met Diego Maradona's Napoli.

The second leg, played in front of a 68,800 capacity crowd in Stuttgart's

Hard earned

THE battle has been won—by Napoli. They are the victors on 5–4 aggregate over Stuttgart, and De Napoli and Giuliani take charge of the UEFA Cup.

Neckar Stadion, was Klinsmann's final game before joining Inter. And fittingly the West German, having returned from suspension, scored Stuttgart's first goal, but it was not enough to prevent a 5–4 aggregate defeat.

Any suggestion that Klinsmann's head would be turned by his new-found status in Italy was dispelled by his refusal to accept a new Mercedes—preferring instead to keep his old-fashioned Volkswagen 'Beetle'—and his reluctance to employ agents, who promised him the world.

He follows his own instincts off the field as well as on it. In less than two years, that policy made Klinsmann a regular choice for West Germany and promised to make him a small fortune in Italy.

There is clearly more to come from this talented player. And it is on his shoulders that West Germany's attacking ambitions will rest when they chase their third consecutive appearance in the World Cup Final in Italy in 1990.

WEST German action men now together with Internazionale of Milan . . . Andreas Brehme (above) and Jurgen Klinsmann on the left, in hot pursuit of the 'Martian' Francini of Napoli in the UEFA Cup Final.

PAUL GASCOIGNE...

? HOME or away, the fans are keeping the turnstiles moving to see the silky skills and cheeky antics of Paul Gascoigne of Tottenham and England. Genius or joker? Sometimes he's both in the same minute or movement.

? The precocious young star has bemused even Spurs manager Terry Venables and Bobby Robson of England by his zany actions on the pitch. As Robson says: 'You need two balls when he plays. One for him and another for the rest of us.'

By ALASTAIR YEOMANS

ABOVE Gascoigne in serious mood against Chile in the Rous Cup of 1989. OPPOSITE Gascoigne in impish mood after a couple of 'interviews' with an unamused referee.

HE is the assured craftsman who, in only his third international appearance, carved his way through the Albanian defence in England's World Cup qualifying match at Wembley in April, 1989, to score the best goal of the game.

He is the youngster who, a few weeks later, took boyish delight in playfully mimicking Peter Shilton while England's goalkeeper was being interviewed by the BBC.

Paul Gascoigne, genius or joker? It is the topic on which everyone in football has an opinion.

BOBBY ROBSON is in no doubt about his ability. The England manager said after the Albanian match: 'The crowd think he is wonderful—and he is. When he almost got into the box, it was like watching George Best.' But Robson added: 'He has to learn to channel some of his talents professionally in team play and show responsibility at the highest levels.

'I enjoyed some of the things he did. But you need two balls when he plays.

Genius or Joker?

One for him and another for the rest of us. I have been in the game for a long time. I have never met anyone with more confidence than this kid.'

DAVID MILLER, sports columnist of *The Times*, speculating on the England line-up of the future, wrote that Gascoigne would be a viable choice 'so long as he can be persuaded not to believe he already possesses the ability of Pelé.'

Gascoigne is still in his early twenties and carries the burden of being one of Britain's highest-ever priced footballers. He displayed his relative immaturity in the 1988–89 season by being booked in eight of his thirty-two appearances for Tottenham Hotspur. He has yet to learn to hide his frustration when he receives unwelcome attention from some of the game's hard men.

BILLY BONDS, West Ham United's faithful warrior, dispelled any thoughts that he plays the game unfairly. After the two had engaged in a midfield battle, Bonds said of Gascoigne: 'If you take away his competitive edge you will destroy him. We had about a dozen tackles together and couple of little tussles, and there was no trouble at all. He's hard but fair, and that's all you could want of anybody.'

Gascoigne's occasional bouts of temperamental behaviour worry the men in charge of him.

DAVE SEXTON, manager of the England 'B' side which played Switzerland in May, 1989, had a warning for the midfield maestro. 'He knows that if he gets into trouble and receives a booking, I will order him off,' declared Sexton before the match. 'Unless you have international experience, you don't realise how easy it is to get booked.'

In the event, Gascoigne's behaviour was impeccable and he scored another magnificent solo goal as England won 2–0.

WILLIE McFAUL, Gascoigne's manager when he was at Newcastle United,

ABOVE Two men with high praise for Gascoigne—Neil Webb, his England team-mate, and Bobby Robson, seen here in happy talk with Poland manager Wojciech Lazarek after England's 3–0 victory in a World Cup qualifying match.

thought his attitude was crucial. 'Self-discipline is what Paul needs most of all,' he said. 'With it, the world can be his oyster. Without it, who knows where he will be in four or five years from now.'

Gascoigne's England colleague NEIL WEBB is impressed with his ball skills. 'His close ball control and dribbling are very good,' he said. 'His first touch is very good and he likes to take people on.'

Liverpool's STEVE McMAHON admires him, too. He says: 'Gascoigne is a very intelligent player. He likes to take control of the ball in commanding positions from where he can distribute it to his team-mates. He seems to enjoy getting among the action and playing short, neat passes rather than sweeping, cross-field ones.'

Chelsea's full-back TONY DORIGO pinpoints the reason why Gascoigne scores so many spectacular goals. He says: 'He has a lot of power in both of his feet, and he's certainly not afraid to have a shot.'

Gascoigne is possibly the most exciting, naturally gifted player to grace the game in Britain since GEORGE BEST. And Best himself is generous in his praise for the young man: 'Gascoigne is the one player in the country who oozes class consistently. He is a fantastic player—the sort the public wants to see.

'There's no doubt he has the chance to be a big star.'

TOP LEFT A couple of contrasting characters are Gascoigne and Vinny Jones, once with Wimbledon and now Leeds. RIGHT Old team-mates of England and Tottenham and Newcastle before that, Gascoigne and Chris Waddle find time for a witty exchange during an international match.

STEVE NICOL

A player of exceptional character

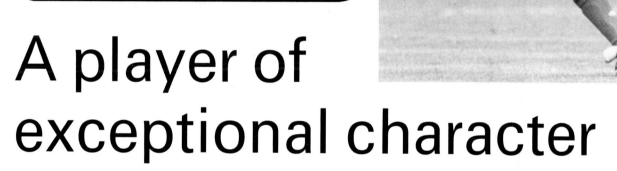

LIVERPOOL endured a traumatic 1988–89 season but one player who emerged as a model of dependability and professionalism was their gritty defender Steve Nicol, voted Player of the Year by the Football Writers Association.

Special circumstances require a special ability to adapt and succeed, an ability which has always marked out Nicol as a player of exceptional character. A full back by inclination, Nicol answered the call at the beginning of the season when central defenders Alan Hansen and Gary Gillespie were injured and Danish international Jan Molby was temporarily unavailable following a court conviction.

The 27-year-old Scot had already proved his versatility by deputising occasionally in midfield the previous season and he made the switch to central defence with remarkable ease. Nicol performed superbly and consistently, sustaining the Liverpool effort during an uncharacteristically fragile beginning to the season.

With his spiky Foreign Legion haircut and size twelve football shoes, Nicol

WHETHER in action for Liverpool or Scotland, Steve Nicol emerges as a model of dependability and professionalism.

. . . AND ANOTHER
PARTY SPOILED

ONE of the happiest moments in an emotional year for Liverpool turned sour when over-exuberant fans invaded the pitch after the Cup Final win over Everton. Goal hero Ian Rush had to run for cover, then the traditional lap of honour had to be abandoned.

can be a decidedly aggressive-looking character, but his appearance belies the true nature of his game which is based on skill and anticipation.

His efforts were acknowledged by Liverpool's manager, Kenny Dalglish, who promoted him to captain when Ronnie Whelan was suspended, and by the English Press, whose votes made him a convincing winner of the Player of the Year award over his nearest rivals, Bryan Robson and Peter Shilton.

'When I think of some of the great names who have won the award—and even some of the people who haven't—it makes me feel very honoured,' says Nicol, the fourth Liverpool player to win the award between 1983 and 1989. The three others were Kenny Dalglish (1983), Ian Rush (1984) and John Barnes (1988).

'Although the honour went to me,' Nicol adds, 'in view of what happened I saw it as a tribute to my family and the entire family of Liverpool. I emerged last season through a strange set of circumstances, with players injured and others not available. But though I have switched about, my true position is full-back and that is where I hope to stay.'

Dalglish needs no convincing about Nicol's worth. 'It's one thing to be able to play in three or four positions but another to play well in all of them,' he says. 'He's a great credit to the club.'

Nor should Nicol's contribution to the Scotland side be overlooked, for that hard-won experience gained with Liverpool pays dividends for the national side.

The Hillsborough tragedy stunned everybody at Anfield but, taking his cue from a dignified and resilient Dalglish, Nicol was foremost among the senior players in the painful period of rehabilitation. Whether it be attending funerals of victims, grieving with the mourning fans or playing with renewed vigour on the pitch, Nicol led by example.

Nicol has been absorbed totally by the Anfield machine since his arrival on Merseyside from Scotland in 1981. He had already made his mark as a teenage professional with Ayr United before his transfer to Liverpool for £300,000. Like many of the club's stars, he started in their Central League side before making his mark in the first team.

His great ability is to perform competently in any position on the field. The football world quickly took notice of his versatility when he scored a hat-trick against Newcastle United at St James's Park in September, 1987, but in Nicol's mind he was simply fulfilling his assigned role of attacking midfielder to the best of his ability.

Between August, 1987, and August, 1989, Nicol missed only one match for Liverpool—the 1988 Charity Shield. Liverpool and Scotland have come to rely on him and he hasn't let them down.

JOHN Barnes in magnificent action as Liverpool of 1989 go all out for the dramatic League-Cup double.

Soccer's darkest day NEXT PAGES ▷

The horror of

■ Saturday, April 15, 1989, was the saddest day in the history of British football. It was a day when the entire nation was plunged into deep shock by the Hillsborough crowd disaster. Ninety-five people died; more than 200 were injured. Many more hundreds who were at the Liverpool–Nottingham Forest match will bear the mental scars for ever.

Nothing can be gained by further detail; the horror of the tragedy is all too vivid still. One can only feel for the bereaved and the permanently incapacitated. And take steps to ensure that it never happens again.

FANS outside the Anfield home of Liverpool in silent homage. On the left is Gerry Marsden paying his emotional tribute at Wembley before the Everton–Liverpool Final with the moving strains of 'You'll Never Walk Alone.'

Hillsborough

POLICE and fans lift trapped spectators to safety.

THE pitch becomes an emergency field dressing station.

FLOWERS and scarves left on the gate at Hillsborough . . .

ARGENTINA BUILD AROUND MARADONA IN HAT-TRICK BID

By KEIR RADNEDGE
(Editor of 'World Soccer')

ARGENTINA footballers know all about the difference between winning and losing. Diego Maradona and Co. found out the hard way after returning home from Spain, in 1982, without the World Cup trophy they had set out to defend.

The squad which had flown from Buenos Aires a few weeks earlier, amid confident hysteria, arrived back to a frosty welcome. Instead of being swept in triumph through passport and baggage checks, all the players found their documents being scrutinised at length and then met customs officials only too ready to open up their suitcases and check a string of undeclared luxury goods.

Manager at the time was Cesar Luis Menotti. Now it is Carlos Salvador Bilardo. But Bilardo has been in football management long enough to know what fate should await him if Argentina return home from Italy next July without the World Cup they won amid such controversial brilliance in Mexico.

Cynics are already claiming that Bilardo's real opinion of Argentina's chances has been revealed by the rumours that, after the finals, he will be staying on in Italy as coach to Maradona's Napoli.

Bilardo, himself, is wrestling with the challenge of rebuilding Argentina despite a host of frustrations. One of those is the absence of most of his top players in Europe. Bilardo made the point most forcibly after Argentina's disappointing showing in an Australian Bicentennial tournament.

He was asked about the pressure he felt as manager of the world champions. Bilardo replied: 'This team was not the World Cup-winning side. The World Cup-winning side played its last game in the Final in Mexico in 1986. That was the end. Now we have to look to the future with new players. Some of them are very good. But World Cup-winners they are not—at least, not at the moment.'

Argentina are, as holders, spared the need to battle through the qualifying rounds to the finals, but Bilardo believes this may be a disadvantage. He says: 'New players need to play serious competitive soccer for the national team. Otherwise they do not gain the experience to cope with the pressures of a

World Cup, and I do not know whether they can take the strain or not.'

Bilardo has not been helped by injuries which have robbed him of even the faint hope of including such as Ricardo Giusti and Jorge Burruchaga in his early preparations.

Giusti was the central defender who converted to right back for the World Cup Finals in Mexico; Burruchaga was the dynamic midfielder who crowned his Mexico campaign by scoring the winning goal in the 3–2 Final win over West Germany. So who are the men on whom Bilardo must rely in Italy?

Maradona will be the key, marked more tightly than ever but very much at home in a football environment which has been his kingdom ever since he left Barcelona for Napoli for a then world record £5 million in 1984. Everything Maradona touches turns to gold; whether that touch is made with foot or hand or any other part of his anatomy.

Bilardo must build a team around Maradona. In goal he can choose between the 1986 veteran Nery Pumpido, now playing for Betis in Spain after recovering from a horrific finger injury, or the hot-tempered Luis Islas. In central defence another 'European' with strong claims is Oscar Ruggeri, another 1986 winner and who is now with Real Madrid.

In midfield the 1986 duo of Sergio Daniel Batista and Hector Enrique may yet be bolstered by the return of Burruchaga—if the French-based schemer can prove he has fully recovered from two serious knee injuries.

Up front, Bilardo's major problem is finding a replacement for the retired Jorge Valdano. Claudio Caniggia of Verona has enormous talent but a controversial reputation and a recent broken leg; Oscar Dertycia says he does not want

the pressure of playing for the national team; Claudio Borghi appears to have lost his way after failing at Milan; and Ramon Diaz has never been as effective for Argentina as he has for a string of Italian clubs, including the 1988–89 champions, Internazionale.

Consider those names carefully. This is the foundation of Bilardo's squad and most of those players are Europe-based. Encapsulated here is Argentina's greatest strength and weakness.

No other country has exported footballers in such numbers. Back as far as the late 1920s, the exodus was alive with stars such as centre-half Luisito Monti and winger Mumo Orsi going to Italy. Spain soon invested heavily in Argentine players. In 1953 Real Madrid signed the man considered by many as the greatest all-round footballer of all time, Alfredo Di Stefano.

The departure of so many players has kept the Argentine domestic game just about solvent but has ruined prospects of World Cup success.

In 1930 Argentina finished runners-up to Uruguay in the inaugural Final in Montevideo. Yet it was not until 1978, on home ground in Buenos Aires, that Argentina finally broke through to victory. Eight years later and Argentina were winners in Mexico, too.

Now for the hat-trick?

OPPOSITE Argentina's manager Carlos Bilardo has a dramatic way of making his point. ABOVE Diego Maradona, the main hope for Argentina in 1990, salutes his Neapolitan worshippers after leading Napoli to victory in the 1989 UEFA Cup.

United have the potential to build a bright future once more with...

ALEX FERGUSON talks about them

MIDWAY through 1988–89 Old Trafford was suddenly filled with life. The imagination of half the city of Manchester had been caught by a football team brimming with panache and flair. The season had begun slowly for United supporters and had ended ignominiously, but for three glorious months it looked as though they were living up to their reputation as the world's most glamorous club.

Remarkably, the anticipation and excitement was not centred in the array of million-pound talent that regularly graces the United turf, but in a crop of eight youngsters whose combined transfer fees would struggle to match Bryan Robson's monthly pay cheque.

Manager Alex Ferguson was confronted with a crippling injury list in the run-up to United's FA Cup tie at Queens Park Rangers in January, 1989. Stars of the calibre of Norman Whiteside, Paul McGrath, Gordon Strachan, Viv Anderson, Colin Gibson and Bryan Robson were all missing from the usual line-up. Ferguson's hand was forced—he had to blood his youngsters.

It was a move that transformed United's season. They performed with verve against Rangers, coming within a minute of a stirring victory, and Ferguson found that he had stumbled on virtue made of necessity.

Russell Beardsmore (20), Lee Sharpe (17), Tony Gill (20), Deiniol Graham (19), Lee Martin (20), Mark Robins (19), David Wilson (19) and Giuliano Maiorana (20) all played their part in the United team during 1989, fuelling optimism

OPPOSITE Proud to wear the red shirt of United . . . one of the new crop of brilliant youngsters at Old Trafford, Deiniol Graham.

FERGIE'S FLEDGLINGS

Report by Des Kelly

in the club's future. Immediately comparisons were drawn with the halcyon days of the 'Busby Babes' era and, with that in mind, the youngsters earned the tag of 'Fergie's Fledglings'. But this irked their manager.

Alex Ferguson said: 'Sir Matt's kids were from a different age and it's never fair to make comparisons like that. It can put unnecessary pressure on them. A lot of the youngsters were put into the side earlier than we would have preferred but, because of their enthusiasm and drive, they have handled the responsibility exceptionally well.

'One of the great things about having a number of home-grown youngsters in a team is that they can nearly always be relied upon to have a fierce loyalty towards the club and a strong sense of unity. They are playing for the jerseys. It's an old saying, but an important one, because they are showing pride not only in themselves but in the club they've been brought up on. And the youngsters make the older players wonder if they'll get back in.'

At this stage Beardsmore and Sharpe appear to be the pick of the bunch, already earning themselves England Under-21 honours.

Sharpe slipped through the scouting nets of many clubs. Birmingham City turned him away at the age of fourteen and West Bromwich Albion advised him to take up the offer of a Youth Training Scheme place at lowly Torquay United, on a salary of £28.50 a week. Ferguson finally stepped in, snapping up Sharpe for a bargain price of £30,000 in April, 1988. He played as cover at left-back for much of his first season, but scouts considered that Sharpe would show his best when he reverts to his favourite role on the left wing.

Beardsmore, a busy midfielder, has fast become a favourite with the United supporters, catching the eye in the dramatic 3–1 victory over Liverpool on New Year's Day, 1989. Trailing to a John Barnes goal, Manchester United looked likely to succumb to their rivals from Merseyside, but Beardsmore set up an equaliser for Brian McClair, presented Mark Hughes with a scoring

chance three minutes later, then fired in the third himself to cap a rousing performance.

Gill had the sizable task of filling the number seven shirt of England skipper Bryan Robson, but it was an opportunity he took with relish, scoring a superb goal in the Cup match at Queens Park Rangers. It marked a spirited comeback for Gill after two Achilles tendon operations and a full year of inactivity.

Others such as Lee Martin would have undoubtedly played more had they not been injured earlier in the season. He too was recruited from junior football as a YTS trainee.

One for the future may be Maiorana, Ferguson's £30,000 signing from Histon, the Eastern Counties League club. 'He is a tricky winger,' said Ferguson, 'with natural ability and is very confident running at defenders. He has good pace and is a good crosser of the ball.'

ABOVE Young Russell Beardsmore in thrilling action against David Platt of Aston Villa.
OPPOSITE Another 'Fergie Fledgling' Lee Martin, who started out as a YTS trainee.

Undoubtedly, the best is yet to come. Ferguson, renowned for his emphasis on youth policies at his former club Aberdeen, has expanded United's local centre of excellence and instituted two more in Belfast and Durham, pledging that 'the production of our own players is now at the core of this club's policy.

'When I took over,' he said, 'United were getting a fair bit of stick from supporters because of the success of Manchester City's youth system. City won the FA Youth Cup a few years ago, mainly with local-born lads, and a high number of these have established themselves as regular first-team players.

'There is no way I can criticise my predecessors. One of the big problems of being in charge of a club like United is that you are under pressure to achieve instant success. But it can be easy to focus attention on immediate rewards at the expense of the long-term future. Moreover, there are probably fewer top-class schoolboy players now than there were twenty years ago.'

In retrospect, the youngsters maintained their dazzling form for only a short time. An FA Cup quarter-final exit at the hands of Nottingham Forest in March, 1989, followed hard on the heels of a crucial League defeat at Norwich City which killed off United's hopes and with it the enthusiasm and inspiration which had made light of the burden placed on the young shoulders.

But the 'fledglings' came of age in that time. They proved capable of soaring to dizzy heights and United have the potential to build a bright future once more.

Continuing the Manchester United theme with a tribute to Sir Matt Busby . . .

THE MAN WHO MADE UNITED GREAT

By DONALD SAUNDERS
*of The Daily Telegraph
with our thanks to
them for permission
to reproduce this
birthday tribute*

THOSE of us who recall the famous image of Frank Swift lying prostrate in his goalmouth after fainting at the end of the 1934 FA Cup Final, find it difficult to accept that Sir Matt Busby is now an octogenarian.

It was this now much loved elder statesman of British soccer who cleared the ball firmly into touch seconds before Swift, a lad of nineteen playing in his first final, collapsed with relief as Manchester City made certain of victory over Portsmouth. Since that memorable afternoon, the name Busby has been

Two of the very great men of the Busby era were George Best, snapped here in heavily-bearded camouflage amidst the foliage, and Bobby Charlton, now an influential member of the United board.

associated with the agony and the ecstasy of young men striving to master the art of football, for their satisfaction and our entertainment.

As we salute Sir Matt today, it is with gratitude for his establishment of a type of football that continues to demonstrate the beauty and excitement of the game, even as a consuming passion for money and success threatens to turn League soccer into a sterile exercise in strength and stamina.

It is not by accident that Manchester United, through whom Sir Matt presented his enlightened vision of the game for nearly a quarter of a century, remain the League's most widely supported club, even though they last won the championship in 1967.

The public at large, whether they stand on the terraces, sit in the stands or follow soccer on their TV screens, like the way Manchester United try to play football and though, during the past two decades, United have been managed by a host of men, as diverse in character as Tommy Docherty and Dave Sexton, they have largely continued to play the Busby way.

When you go to Old Trafford, or to any ground where United are appearing, you know you are likely to see players whose artistry will shine through even the drabbest match. Sir Matt's belief that soccer is a simple though beautiful game, to be enjoyed by players and spectators, was shared during the Fifties and Sixties by such other far-seeing managers as Ron Greenwood, Bill Nicholson and the Joe Mercer-Malcolm Allison partnership.

As he reaches the grand old age of eighty, United's venerable President must be pleased to note that this philosophy is now regaining popularity within the First Division after twenty years during which only United and the West Ham of John Lyall's days remained consistently faithful.

In recent seasons, Kenny Dalglish has turned Liverpool into an entertaining,

as well as a successful team, and George Graham has removed the label of 'boring' from Arsenal's jersey. Meanwhile Brian Clough, once an impudent young critic of Sir Matt, is currently fielding his most exciting Nottingham Forest side and Terry Venables is regaining for Tottenham the reputation for entertainment they enjoyed in the Sixties.

But the greatest satisfaction for Sir Matt has been the recent award to Alex Ferguson of another two-year contract as United's manager, despite their failure to win anything under him so far. Mr Ferguson is a firm believer in the Busby philosophy. Given time, he might also provide the successful team for which some younger supporters are now impatient.

These youngsters were not around to see Sir Matt take over United at the end of the Second World War and transform them into one of the most readily recognised names in the entire world of sport. So they would not understand why foreigners, overhearing the conversation of British tourists, so often make the seemingly bizarre interruption 'Manchester United—Bobby Charlton.'

Yet, Sir Matt's great influence on British sport might have been lost forever if his widowed mother's plan to emigrate with him to the United States in the Twenties had not fallen through. And if Louis Rocca, then United's chief scout, had not written to him in the closing weeks of the last war, disclosing the availability of 'a great job,' Busby might instead have been building outstanding football teams at Anfield.

In 1936 Sir Matt, a wing-half of rare skill, moved from Manchester City to Liverpool who, as his wartime service came to a close, invited him to return as their chief coach. Instead Sir Matt, on demobilisation in September, 1945, became United's manager. During the next 24 years, three great teams represented Manchester United. They won the championship five times, finished second in seven further seasons, took part in four FA Cup Finals—twice winning—and became the first English club to win the European Cup in 1968.

The names of players who wore United's red jersey with such distinction in that glorious period now read like the register of soccer's aristocracy.

To mention just a few, there are Johnny Carey, Jack Rowley and Johnny Morris from the 1948 FA Cup-winning team; Roger Byrne, Duncan Edwards and Tommy Taylor, who died at Munich with five other members of the 1958 squad that surely would have conquered Europe; and Bobby Charlton, Denis Law and George Best, who helped carry United right to the top again ten years later.

How, we might ask, did Sir Matt come to achieve all this at one club? The answer, I suspect, is contained in a few sentences of his modest biography. 'Long before I became established, long before I was captain of Scotland, long before I moved from Manchester City to Liverpool,' he wrote in 1973, 'I vowed that if ever I became a manager, I would respect players as individuals, who needed individual treatment and thereby try to inspire respect for them.'

Sir Matt has far exceeded that objective. He has earned the affection as well as the respect of all of us who, as player or spectator, have been part of the illustrious post-war history of Manchester United.

Lawyer Gudni's trial is over . . .

By PETER DRURY

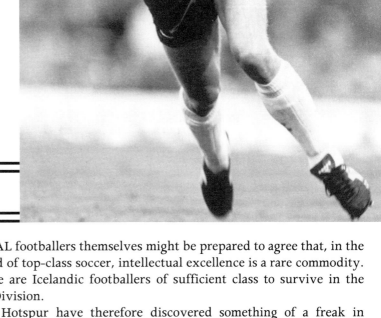

PROFESSIONAL footballers themselves might be prepared to agree that, in the physical world of top-class soccer, intellectual excellence is a rare commodity. Almost as rare are Icelandic footballers of sufficient class to survive in the English First Division.

Tottenham Hotspur have therefore discovered something of a freak in defender Gudni Bergsson, a bright law student with a sharp footballing brain who hails from the distant footballing outpost of Reykjavik.

Bergsson, an affable young man, had represented Iceland more than twenty times before reaching his mid-twenties but, like most of his footballing compatriots, he seemed certain to spend his career in relative international anonymity. The same accolades that are afforded to the Gary Linekers, Ruud Gullits and Diego Maradonas of this world rarely reach the humble stars of Iceland.

Bergsson was in the fourth year of five, reading Legal Studies at Reykjavik University, and a comfortable living from a 'safe' and respectable profession seemed assured when Spurs' manager Terry Venables stepped in in November, 1988, to throw his world into exciting confusion. At the time, Bergsson was

Bergsson has no need to feel the lonely stranger at White Hart Lane. Here are two of his 'import' colleagues, Mohamed Ali Amar (better known as Nayim) and goalkeeper Eric Thorsvedt.

playing his football with local amateur side Valur Reykjavik, as well as fulfilling the traditional sweeper's role in the national side. But Venables invited him to White Hart Lane on trial and he felt unable to turn down the offer.

It was not that he considered his legal studies to be unimportant—indeed, in the fulness of time, he expects to return to them—but he knew that, while they could wait, football could not. So, his legal training was suspended and he jumped on the first available 'plane to London.

Delighted by the opportunity to try and prove himself in a recognised footballing nation, Bergsson was surprised only that it was an English club which had approached him. Aston Villa, under Graham Turner, once offered him a trial which came to nothing. In his dreams, it had always been a Continental side from, say, West Germany for whom he would play—not because of any preference, but because he knew that English clubs rarely employed a sweeper system.

Bergsson quickly made a good impression in North London and, on Boxing Day, 1988, having played just a handful of reserve-team games, he was thrown into action against Luton Town. Being an amateur, he had not had to wrestle with the problem of work permits, but as the Luton match wore on, it became increasingly evident that Venables would want to snap him up as a full-time professional. His performance was stylish and assured—everything a Tottenham player should be.

He went on to play a string of games in the First Division, the most important of which was the North London Derby against Arsenal, a match which produced an atmosphere the like of which he had never before experienced. It was a credit to the wise head on his relatively young shoulders that he strolled through it with authority.

His opinion of the English game was unaffected by his personal involvement and he said : 'I have always had a high opinion of English football. Obviously the standard of football is of a higher standard than it was in Iceland. The game is much faster—even more intense than the internationals I have played. The competition and pace at which you are closed down and must respond is also incredible and you have to adapt very quickly or you are lost.

'Yet I have not been surprised at any of that because I have followed, and watched on television, the English game since I was a youngster. I have also played against English club sides so I knew what to expect.'

Although, by the end of the 1988–89 season, Bergsson had played only nine first-team games for Tottenham, it was clear that he was a player capable of

'The English game is much faster – more intense than our internationals'

Welcome to White Hart

GARY Lineker is back in England with Tottenham Hotspur, thanks to Terry Venables, his old manager at Barcelona. And here is Gary's fond farewell (he's on the extreme right) after Barcelona's defeat of Sampdoria in the Cup-Winners' Cup Final of 1989.

holding his own at that star-studded club. He had earned a regular place in a squad which included England 'flair' players Paul Gascoigne and Chris Waddle, as well as fellow-imports in the Norwegian goalkeeper Eric Thorsvedt and the Spaniard Nayim.

Cosmopolitan Tottenham is an exciting place to be at the moment, whichever nationality you happen to be. But for a trainee lawyer from Reykjavik, it is a wonderful bonus of which he is firmly intent to make the most.

Au revoir, Chris

IT'S farewell and the best of French fortune to Chris Waddle of Spurs on joining Marseille. But he should still be available for England—as he was here in high-speed action against the Hungarian defender he left flat-footed. Now he is on his way to his first million after his £4.5 million transfer to the top French club with seemingly bottomless pockets.

RUSSIANS⸻
LOOK AHEAD

RUSSIANS Oleg Protasov (left) and Igor Belanov (below) are spearheading the Soviet Union's push into the 1990s. These sparkling individuals are providing as much a revelation on the field as President Gorbachev's social reforms have been off it.

Protasov, a prolific goalscorer, is stretching the limits of excellence that were once the sole pursuit of the great Oleg Blokhin. Protasov set an all-time record of thirty-five goals in thirty-four games for Dnepr in 1985 and has inherited Blokhin's revered status in Soviet football.

Belanov, the 1986 European Footballer of the Year, was the Soviet's outstanding player in the Mexico World Cup Finals, the highlight being his breathtaking hat-trick against Belgium.

Such skill and genius will only further the policies of *glasnost* and *perestroika*.

NAT'S FIFTY YEARS OF DEVOTION

Some golden memories of the old 'Lion of Vienna'

By MIKE NALLY (The Observer)

NAT LOFTHOUSE is bracing himself for a season-long shindig to celebrate his golden jubilee with Bolton Wanderers.

The word at Burnden Park is that the stocky frame that withstood the some-times cruel attention of defenders at all levels of the game for more than two decades will be battered again by the generosity of a legion of admirers. Loft-house, now sixty-three, is anticipating the challenge with characteristic forti-tude and modesty, welcoming it as a tribute to the club to which he has been devoted for fifty years.

Taking a breather from his duties as manager of the executive suite at the Park, he said : 'I don't look at it like they're all going to be talking about 'Lofty'. They're going to be on about the Wanderers. You can't have me without them. It's the same as for Tom Finney and Bobby Charlton and their clubs, you see. We belong.'

Such sentiments, and his no-nonsense approach as a player and in a variety of back-room jobs since retirement, confirm him as a symbol of the game at a time when it seems in retrospect to have been innocent.

It was never innocent, of course, not even in the pre-League days, when the Wanderers were known as Christ Church and played on Dick Cockle's Field. And he is quick to counsel against romanticism.

'Football had to develop. But there's too much 'method' on the pitch and

'Football had to develop . . . but the style's gone, and so's the loyalty'

too much money behind the scenes. The style's gone, and so's the loyalty.'

Lofthouse cut a less than combative figure when he signed as an amateur in 1939 after impressive performances for Bolton Schools; he was handicapped by lack of speed and strength. The latter was remedied when he worked down the pit as a Bevin Boy during the war. 'It made me tough. I lost a lot of puppy fat . . . and I was working with some of the finest guys on earth, those miners. I thought how bloody lucky I was to look forward to being a footballer and not that full-time.'

He signed professional forms immediately after the war ended, going on to play 452 League matches for the Wanderers (in which he scored 255 goals) and thirty-three internationals for England (in which he scored thirty). He played in two FA Cup Finals, in 1953 and 1958. The Wanderers lost to Blackpool 3–4 in the first, the so-called Matthews Final, but Lofthouse scored and was named Footballer of the Year. They beat Manchester United 2–0 in the second, remembered for his belligerence in bundling Harry Gregg into the net with the ball for the second and deciding goal.

He is best remembered as an international for his performance in Austria in 1952, a match billed as the Championship of Europe. He scored twice again

THE DAY MORTY

By WILLIAM JOHNSON (Daily Telegraph)

NAT LOFTHOUSE, who as president of Bolton Wanderers is in his fiftieth year of outstanding and loyal service at Burnden Park, counts the two Stans from Blackpool—Matthews and Mortensen—among the best friends he has made during a sparkling football career.

Yet he still finds it hard to grasp why writers of football folklore refer to one of the most memorable matches in Wembley history (May 2, 1953) as the Matthews Cup Final.

'To this day I would still politely disagree with anybody who gives it that title,' he declared. 'There was a lot of emotion about a winners' medal for Matthews after two near misses and he had a tremendous match that day.

'When a guy like Matthews hit his best form on a stage like that, I don't think a bullet could have stopped him. But what about Morty? The first player to score a hat-trick in a Wembley final—and what a hat-trick.'

Mr Lofthouse reasoned that Sir Stanley would be the first to admit that it was a magnificent all-round effort by Blackpool to overcome what had seemed a hopeless cause, a 3–1 deficit with only seventeen minutes remaining.

as England won 3–2, surviving another goalmouth collision for another clincher. He was known as the Lion of Vienna from then on.

Lofthouse doubts that he would be such an effective player in the modern game. 'I don't think I could have played in the formation they use today. The guy in the middle is on his own, no wingers to speak of. As far as trapping or working the ball goes, I wasn't too good. But if I had it straight, I could use it, and I could jump a bit.

'And I was damned lucky with the guys I played with in the big matches. Wilf Mannion would get it, say, and he'd give it to Tom Finney or Stan Matthews, and they knew what to do with it.' His peers suggest that he under-rates himself. Finney recalls his positioning and tenacity; Jackie Milburn respected him as a canny rival for the England place.

His blackest memory is of the FA Cup match against Stoke City at the Park in 1946, when barriers collapsed and thirty-three spectators died. His greatest regret is the decline of the Wanderers, who were in the top half of the First Division when he joined them and now languish in the Third. He prefers not to be quoted on that.

He retired because of injury at the end of 1959–60, but returned the next

TOM Finney of unforgettable England fame. The famous man of Preston recalls Lofthouse's tenacity and positional ability.

GOT IT WRONG...

An indication of the camaraderie at that time between two of England's best forwards was the comment by Mortensen to Lofthouse at half-time.

'He said "congratulations" to me,' recalled Lofthouse. 'I told him it was a bit early for that—we hadn't won yet—but he reminded me that I had scored in every round of the Cup. That still gives me a thrill.'

Mortensen took up the story for those thrilling closing minutes. 'We got a free kick and Ernie Taylor asked me what I was going to do with it. I told him it was getting desperate and I was going to have a bang at goal, even though it was outside the penalty area.

'It went in and that gave us the inspiration to look for the equaliser. I managed to score that one as well, but I wasn't thinking of the hat-trick. All I was concerned about was going on to win the Cup.

'That was when Stan stepped in. He had been threatening all afternoon and eventually he got over the perfect cross for Bill Perry to shoot home the winner.

'I don't think any of us cared who had been the hero of the hour. My main concern was the public of Blackpool. They had come down with us for two other finals in five years and at last they had something to celebrate.'

THANKS .. to both *The Daily Telegraph* and *The Observer* for kindly permitting us to print the tributes to Lofthouse.

'LOFTY' – THE PIED PIPER OF BOLTON

WHEN Nat Lofthouse was on the run, it seemed that every youngster in Bolton would follow him to the ends of the earth. This was just a fitness try-out, but still the young autograph-hunters were up with their leader.

season to play at inside-right when the Wanderers beat Manchester City 3–1 at home. Alongside him that afternoon was a promising winger, Francis Lee, then sixteen.

Percy M. Young, a shrewd fan, rhapsodised about that performance in a beguiling history of the Wanderers, published in 1961:

'Lofthouse's function was tutorial—to see the boy through the rigours of a local derby. The manner in which he conducted his function, now counselling, now encouraging, now putting the ball across for the outside-right to get a feel of it, was an inspiration: here was a player who cared for the game, for the club and for the future . . . There is English football; there are English footballers; and Lofthouse is, perhaps, in our time the most English of them all.'

The star who divided a city . . .

MO Johnston in action for Scotland.

TRANSFER sensation of the decade was that of Mo Johnston, the former Celtic idol, to Rangers. Graeme Souness, manager of Rangers, had signed a Catholic! Glasgow knew no other topic of conversation for months. And yet there was wry humour emerging from the controversy, including that of the Celtic fan who re-named his fourth son so that he had Eeny, Meeny, Miney and Billy.

IFB concentrates on the football skills of Johnston as JASON TOMAS of the *Sunday Times* examines the files of the Scotland forward and recalls what others say of the international striker and record-breaker.

'I am a wiser person now'

MO JOHNSTON can never have been studied more closely and critically than he was on April 26, 1989. That night, he scored one of the goals in a 2–1 win over Cyprus at Hampden to bring his World Cup total to eight and break the Scotland record established by Kenny Dalglish and Joe Jordan.

Among those watching him reach that was Malcolm Macdonald, the former Newcastle, Arsenal and England centre-forward, and one of the most perceptive analysts of the esoteric goalscoring art.

Macdonald, it will be recalled, scored all England's goals when they thrashed Cyprus 5–0 at Wembley in 1975, and had previously seen Johnston playing for Scotland only on television. The experience of getting a clearer view has

RANGERS' manager
Graeme Souness (above)
always ready to explain to
Ibrox fans the reasons for
his moves.

convinced him that Johnston's reputation as one of Europe's best strikers is not exaggerated.

Johnston's goal against Cyprus—a spectacular overhead kick—reminded Macdonald of 'Denis Law at his best.' Although some were disappointed that Johnston didn't get more goals, Macdonald points out that Cyprus have improved considerably since he demolished them, and that Johnston's team-mates made it difficult for him because they lacked composure.

Macdonald, indeed, has no hesitation in putting Johnston in the same category as England's Gary Lineker. 'Lineker is possibly a better finisher,' Macdonald argues, 'but I think Johnston covers more ground, and the types of goals he tends to get are more varied.

'He and Ally McCoist (*his Scotland striking partner*) appear to have been exceptionally well educated. They have an excellent appreciation of the basics of the job, like positioning and timing. At first glance, they seem too much alike, certainly physically. But my impression of them is that McCoist is a footballer who scores a few goals, while Johnston is a scorer who plays a bit of football.'

The first time that Johnston was drawn to Macdonald's attention was when the latter was Fulham's manager and Johnston was a part-timer with Partick Thistle. Johnston was recommended to Macdonald by a Scottish scout, but Macdonald was put off by the reports of the youngster's irresponsible streak.

This factor has always troubled those who have worked with Johnston, a gregarious, fun-loving character whose social life in Britain—Glasgow especially—made him the tabloids' delight. In terms of his lifestyle, he trod the same path as Charlie Nicholas and Frank McAvennie, two of his closest friends. For some time, he seemed destined to be remembered more for reports on what he got up to off the field than for his usually vibrant performances on it.

In this respect, Johnston, who did as well at Watford and Celtic as he did at Partick, had to pay a heavy price for his immaturity in 1986. Having landed in trouble because of an incident during Scotland's World Cup qualifying trip to Australia, he was left out of the squad for the finals of the competition in Mexico.

Alex Ferguson, then Scotland's caretaker manager, makes no apologies for the decision, despite the fact that the Scots scored only once in their three Mexico ties. Referring to the off-the-field problems which undermined Scotland's 1978 World Cup challenge in Argentina, he explains: 'I was under a lot of pressure to make sure that there was no repeat of these. I was taking a bit of a chance as it was in selecting Nicholas and McAvennie—I felt that having Johnston as well was asking for trouble.'

Ferguson, however, acknowledges that Johnston, twenty-seven, has matured considerably since then. Johnston himself attributes this to the responsibilities of being a father—he has a daughter—and his move to Nantes in June, 1987. Johnston admits that he found it difficult earlier in his career to come to terms with being a big name in a hotbed football city such as Glasgow. 'I didn't help myself because I was going out all the time. But I am a wiser person now.

'When I left for France, I had to contemplate failure for the first time because I was going into a totally different environment. It was not wanting to be branded a flop that made me alter my lifestyle—I badly wanted to disprove the people who were expecting me to fall flat on my face.'

Johnston's attitude certainly stood him in good stead during the 1988–89 season, after he virtually destroyed France's hopes of reaching the 1990 World Cup Finals by getting both goals in a 2–0 Scotland win. Not surprisingly, that hardly endeared him to the French public, as reflected by the boos he attracted when playing for Nantes and the hate mail he received.

Working abroad has also helped Johnston improve his technical ability. There is a parallel here in the case of Gary Lineker.

LIKE LINEKER, Johnston has always had tremendous pace, and been particularly effective when chasing balls hit into the space behind opposing defences.

LIKE LINEKER, the experience of playing in a more studious environment, where there are fewer matches and a greater emphasis on polishing ball-skills in training, has enabled him to improve his first touch and tactical awareness.

As for his success at international level, there is no doubt that Johnston has owed much to Ally McCoist, a player with a similar temperament and personality. 'They relate well to each other,' says Scotland's coach Andy Roxburgh, almost like a headmaster talking about a pair of boisterous, mischievous schoolboys.

One example could be seen in Scotland's win over France, when the ball was pumped towards the French area and McCoist made an excellent run to force a French defender into a poor clearance. The ball broke to Steve Nicol and from his cross Johnston scored the second 'killer' goal.

There was an equally intriguing example in Scotland's victory over Cyprus. On the rare occasion that McCoist failed to get into a position to stop a Cypriot defender playing the ball back to his 'keeper, Johnston was ready to run from the other side of the field to do the job for him.

As Roxburgh points out, Johnston has not allowed his personal success to undermine his sense of responsibility towards his colleagues. 'In many ways, he and McCoist emphasise the camaraderie and sense of unity running through our squad,' Roxburgh enthuses.

Scotland have not been slow to recognise the psychological advantage of having strikers of this calibre. When they kick off, it is not unusual to see them just belt the ball deep into the opposition's half. 'We actually practise it in training,' Roxburgh says. 'We do it to demonstrate our attitude—to show our intent.'

Not for nothing is the ball usually directed towards Mo Johnston.

JUBILANT Celtic players celebrate their remarkable Scottish Cup Final triumph over Rangers in 1989, with Roy Aitken hoisting high the trophy.

By Brendan
Gallagher

WOMEN'S FOOTBALL IS ALIVE AND WELL

WOMEN'S football in England is finally shedding its Cinderella image and is rapidly emerging as a game well worth playing—and watching!

More than 2,300,000 viewers watched the 1989 Women's FA Cup Final between Leasowe Pacific, from Liverpool, and the Friends of Fulham. The Liverpool girls won an emotional 3–2 victory at Old Trafford, just a week after the Hillsborough Disaster, and the high quality of the football gave much-needed credibility to the women's game in Britain.

'The Women's Cup Final gave us excellent viewing figures, on a par with our American football coverage, and the audience response was tremendous,' said Channel Four's Commissioning Editor for Sport, Mike Miller.

'As a sportsman I was impressed with the match as a spectacle. The game is slower than the men's professional game, but the skills are good, there are no boring offside tactics, no dissent and lots of goals. If it can be more widely introduced at schools level and with more exposure, it should take off.'

Women's football is already big business in Scandinavia and Italy, where the best players are semi-professional and key matches are regularly televised live. England striker Kerry Davies has already tried her luck in Italy, playing for a factory team in Naples, and more could follow.

There are currently 8,000 women footballers in England, with 250 registered clubs in twenty-one leagues. They represent the tip of the iceberg and the potential for improvement and development is vast, especially if a sympathetic sponsor can be found.

Women's football in England first came to prominence during World War One, when teams of factory workers played matches to raise money for war charities. Perhaps the most famous was Dick Kerr's XI, from the big engineering

THERE is nothing gimmicky about women's football at national level—as the pictures of their 1989 Cup Final at Old Trafford illustrate. The winners were Leasowe Pacific, of Liverpool, by the odd goal of a five-goal thriller against Friends of Fulham.

works in Preston, which was finally disbanded in 1965 after 800 charity matches.

The women's game made no significant developments until England's World Cup victory of 1966, an event which galvanised the sport in this country at all levels, women included.

Playing numbers increased and, in 1969, the Women's Football Association was formed to administer the sport. Another breakthrough came the following year when the Football Association gave permission for the girls to play on FA pitches and for FA referees to officiate.

The first WFA Final was held in 1971, Southampton beating Westholme United 2–1 and, the following year, England played their first international when they beat Scotland 3–2 at Ravenscraig Stadium, Greenock. Since then England have played all over the world, with internationals in Holland, Norway, Sweden, Finland, Belgium, Eire, West Germany, USA and even Japan.

Possibly the outstanding result was in 1988, when England travelled to Italy and astounded the critics by winning the *Mundialito* (Mini World Cup). England started with a draw against France, then defeated USA 2–0 to qualify for the final against the highly-ranked Italians, who develop their skills in their powerful professional league comprising twenty-four clubs.

England won 2–1 in extra time, a victory which resulted in the side being voted as Women's Sports Team of the Year by the *Sunday Times*. It was a result that gave valuable momentum to women's football and the future looks bright.

Women's football has proved it can attract a wide television audience and more widespread coverage seems likely. The sponsors are beginning to show a serious interest.

As they say in the States, it could become a whole new ball game!

. . . and the last word to the ladies with a near miss!